Twayne's English Authors Series

EDITOR OF THIS VOLUME

Sarah W. R. Smith, Tufts University

John Clare

TEAS 312

John Clare by W. Hilton

(Courtesy of the National Portrait Gallery, London)

JOHN CLARE

By William Howard

University of Regina

TWAYNE PUBLISHERS
A DIVISION OF G. K. HALL & CO., BOSTON

Published in 1981 by Twayne Publishers,
A Division of G. K. Hall & Co.
All Rights Reserved

Printed on permanent/durable acid-free paper and bound
in the United States of America

First Printing

Library of Congress Cataloging in Publication Data

Howard, William James.
    John Clare.

    (Twayne's English authors series ; TEAS 312)
    Bibliography: p. 198-201
    Includes index.
    1.   Clare, John, 1793-1864—Criticism and interpre-
tation.
PR4453.C6Z73   821'.3   80-19278
ISBN 0-8057-6734-7

Contents

About the Author

William Howard teaches poetry and fiction of the Romantic Period at the University of Regina. He developed his interest in John Clare while studying for his Master's degree at the University of British Columbia and while travelling in England during his Ph.D. studies at the University of Leeds. He is the editor of *Wascana Review* and author of articles on Maria Edgeworth and Sir Walter Scott.

Preface

The true extent of Clare's genius lies obscured in the manuscript vaults of museums and libraries on both sides of the Atlantic. Partially owing to shifting fashion in early nineteenth-century poetry, but primarily to his personal misfortune of spending the last twenty-four years of his life in mental asylums, most of his mature work was not published during his lifetime. Much has yet to appear in print. Occasionally since his death, though, glimpses of his genius have been provided by several biographies; by new editions of his poems, letters, and prose; as well as by critical books and articles that have explored material not readily available to the public. This book attempts to examine his work in a light that will complement C. Day Lewis's study of his lyric impulse, John Barrell's examination of his sense of place, Mark Storey's study of his debt to the poetic tradition of the late eighteenth century, and the valuable work of others too numerous to mention.

The emphasis here will be on Clare's own statements about his method of composing poetry and on how those comments illuminate his practice in individual poems. Rather than as a theoretical framework that would encompass all his diverse modes of expression, however, those statements will be used as one of several possible keys to an understanding of what I consider to be his most characteristic verse, that which grew out of his direct contemplation of his natural environment. Thus, I look at the poems' form rather than their philosophy or their place in a particular tradition. It will become clear from the second chapter, however, that I see him as primarily a Romantic poet, though like all the Romantics he owed a great deal to the previous century.

The personal response to Clare that has sustained my interest in this study is a persistent admiration for his dedication to the profession of poet. Reading over the thousands of pages of manuscript that Clare has left us, no one could escape the conviction that he took this role seriously, that he was not a farm laborer who spent his spare time writing, but a man who unashamedly believed his purpose in life was to write poetry even though he had to supplement his meager income by working in the fields. He would have approved the now infamous words of the doctor who committed him to the Northampton asylum that he had spent years "addicted to Poetical prosing." Such a poet deserves to be taken seriously, not because his personal circumstances made his profession difficult, but because once we surmount the barrier of sympathy that any perusal of his biography is sure to elicit, we find a sensitive and intelligent man who wrote and thought about poetry with single-minded dedication for over fifty years.

Unfortunately, much of what he said has been corrupted by careless or misguided editing, beginning with his first publisher and continuing, with a few exceptions, into the last decade. To overcome the problem of finding a reliable text that is readily available to the reader of this book, I have used Eric Robinson and Geoffrey Summerfield's admirable editions, whenever possible. Otherwise poems have been quoted directly from the manuscripts (but substituting "ands" for ampersands in the poetry) and accompanied by a note giving the most dependable published source. This method not only allows the reader to compare Clare's original words with the consistently unreliable text of J. W. Tibble's *The Poems of John Clare* and the frequently inaccurate *Poems of John Clare's Madness* edited by Geoffrey Grigson, but also ensures that Clare will be read as he wrote. As a result, Clare speaks in his own idiom, with little punctuation and with his own spelling and dialect vocabulary intact. With Clare, more than with most poets, the reader must participate in the creation of the poem in order to appreciate the poet's distinctive voice.

WILLIAM HOWARD

University of Regina

Acknowledgments

I am especially indebted to Craig Miller for sparking my interest in the Romantic poets and for introducing me to John Clare. For allowing me permission to quote from the transcripts for his forthcoming Oxford English Texts edition of Clare's works, I am grateful to Eric Robinson, as I am to Margaret Grainger and David Powell for their assistance in checking the accuracy of these quotations. The cooperation of Tony Cross and his staff at the Peterborough Museum and of the staff at the Northampton Public Library and the Bodleian Library made my work not only more accurate, but more enjoyable. Finally, I am indebted to Christopher Murray for his editorial help, my wife and family for their patience, Mark Storey for aid in locating material, Gisela Fiege for typing the final draft, and the President's Fund of the University of Regina for its generous financial assistance.

Chronology

1793   July 13. John, first child and only son of Parker and Anne Clare, born at Helpston, Northamptonshire.

1806   Bought his first books, Dr. Watts's *Hymns and Spiritual Songs* and James Thomson's *Seasons.*

1809   Act of Enclosure passed for the area including Helpston. Worked for Francis Gregory at The Blue Bell Inn, the "nursery for that lonely & solitary musing which ended in rhyme."

1814   Bought his first notebook and began recording his poems in it.

1819   Met John Taylor, his eventual publisher.

1820   Jan. 16. *Poems Descriptive of Rural Life and Scenery* published by Taylor and Hessey, and E. Drury. It was an instant success, going through four editions that year. March. First visit to London where he met several leading literary and artistic figures of the day. March 16. Married Martha (Patty) Turner.

1821   Joined the group of regular contributors to Taylor's recently purchased *London Magazine.* September. *The Village Minstrel, and Other Poems* published in two volumes by Taylor and Hessey, and E. Drury.

1822   May–June. Second visit to London where he met Hazlitt, Lamb, Hood, and J. H. Reynolds.

1824   May. Third visit to London, this time to see Dr. Darling for treatment. Met DeQuincey, Coleridge, and George Darley. July 14. Viewed Byron's funeral cortège as it crossed London.

1825   Nov. His essay on "Popularity in Authorship" published in *European Magazine.*

1827   *The Shepherd's Calendar: With Village Stories, and Other Poems* published by James Duncan for John Taylor.

1828   Feb. Fourth visit to London, again for treatment by Dr. Darling.

1830   July. Publicly cursed Shylock in a Peterborough performance of *The Merchant of Venice*. This incident was
followed by a period of severe illness.

1832   May. Moved from Helpston to a new cottage at Northborough.

1835   *The Rural Muse* published by Whittaker and Co.

1837   Committed to Dr. Matthew Allen's asylum at High Beech,
Essex.

1841   July. Escaped from High Beech and walked eighty miles
home in four days. Remained at home until Dec. 29 when
he was taken to the Northampton General Lunatic
Asylum.

1844   In the same town, but unknown to each other, Clare and
Wordsworth watched the Royal Progress of Queen
Victoria and Prince Albert through Northampton.

1845   W. F. Knight began collecting and transcribing the poems
Clare wrote at Northampton.

1864   May 20. Clare died peacefully at the Northampton
asylum.

CHAPTER 1

Clare's Life

JOHN Clare was born on July 13, 1793, five years after Byron, a year after Shelley, and two years before Keats. Clare's career bore few similarities to those of his great contemporaries; he had only a rudimentary education, he lacked the encouragement to write poetry that their social positions provided, and he did not have their early knowledge of the literary world or opportunities for travel. His first book, published in 1820, provided the public with its last love affair with a Romantic poet, but it appeared long after the other three had established their reputations. By the end of that year Keats had published all of the work that was to appear in his lifetime, Byron had followed the major success of *Childe Harold* with the first two cantos of *Don Juan,* and most of Shelley's major work, with the exception of "Adonais," had already made its way into print. Three years later Clare was the lone survivor of the four. Although he continued to write poetry into the age of Tennyson, Browning, and Arnold, the popular and critical success of his first book was never repeated and he spent the last third of his life without a reading public. He died in a Northampton asylum in 1864.

He was born into poverty, the son of an agricultural day-laborer, Parker Clare, and his wife Ann, in what he was later to call the "gloomy village" of Helpston, Northamptonshire.[1] A twin sister died almost at birth, but another sister, Sophia, completed the family in 1798. Theirs was a reasonably independent existence in the early years of his life even though the family relied for subsistence on casual labor and the sale of apples from a single tree on their rented property. Both parents were dedicated to their children: Parker Clare introduced his son not only to field labor, but to the mental storehouse of ballads and songs which were to form the basis of much of his later literary development, and Ann Clare encouraged his ambitions to

13

become a scholar. Their success can be measured by their son's career and by his enduring affection for them: "I have every reason to turn to their memories with the warmest feelings of gratitude, and satisfaction," he wrote in 1821.[2] Clare supported them for the rest of their lives; he eventually became the primary bread winner when first his mother became seriously ill, with dropsy, and then his father, with rheumatism.

Neither the Clares' poverty nor the gloom of the village seems to have prevented the children from an essentially happy and carefree childhood. In "The Village Minstrel" and elsewhere Clare emphasizes his solitude and loneliness as a boy, but he also indicates that the solitary tending of sheep and cows, or hunting for birds' nests, or fishing, were a source of pleasure to him. In contrast, too, accounts of his boyhood reveal an intimate knowledge of children's communal games and the names of several friends who shared in these activities. Even the numerous poems that detail his recollections of childhood consistently stress the contrast between the joys of early life and the torment of his adult years.

From age seven to twelve he attended a day school at Glinton, a neighboring village, for at least three months of the year. Here he learned to read and write and was stimulated to explore other avenues of learning, even, it seems, to flirt with the possibility of a teaching career. When forced to seek permanent employment he continued to study first at a Glinton night school and later informally with other boys in the area. His childhood reading was eclectic, embracing such titles as *Robin Hood's Garland,* Izaac Walton's *The Compleat Angler,* one of John Abercrombie's books on gardening, and *Robinson Crusoe.* In later life the influence of these years was reflected in his avid reading of newspapers and periodicals as well as in his constant requests for the loan of books from his friends.

Born into the circumstances that he was, however, he soon discovered that his education and enquiring mind were not sufficient to find him steady employment near Helpston and the family that was increasingly dependent on him. The search for a suitable occupation was Clare's most serious problem as a youth, partly because of the difficulty of finding work that was not too strenuous for his constitution and partly because of his self-confessed diffidence. He tried gardening briefly, shoemaking even more briefly, and was sent to several potential benefactors with the hope of obtaining a position in a wealthy household, but to no avail. "The fact was I felt timid & fearful of undertaking the first trial in everything," he wrote; "they would not urge me to anything against my will so I livd on at home taking work as it fell."[3] Since he overcame this timidity in his attempts to have his first poems published, and since he seems to have flourished at the two jobs that allowed him leisure to write (ploughing or tending horses for his neighbor Francis Gregory and burning lime at various locations) a more likely explanation might be that he increasingly felt a conflict between the necessity for gaining an occupation and his secret desire to make his living by writing poetry.

He had begun writing verse after reading James Thomson's *Seasons* in a copy loaned to him by one of the local boys. He credits Thomson's opening lines to Spring with inspiring him to purchase the poem, which he did with some difficulty a week later. On his return from his second attempt to buy the book, as he records in one of his autobiographical sketches,

. . . the sun got up, and it was a beautiful morning; I could not wait till I got back without reading it, and as I did not like to let anybody see me reading on the road of a working day, I clumb over the wall into Burghley Park, and nestled in a lawn at the wall side. The scenery around me was uncommonly beautiful at that time of the year, and what with reading the book, and beholding the beauties of artful nature in the park, I got into a strain of descriptive rhyming in my journey home. This was 'The Morning Walk,' the first thing I committed to paper.[4]

His compositions multiplied under the convenience of Francis Gregory's employ and the criticism of his parents. This criticism was solicited by reading what he claimed were the songs and poems of accomplished poets aloud to his parents for their opinion. In reality they were his own compositions which he revised, destroyed, or hoarded as they met with favor or censure. Even at this age—he was about sixteen—his dedication to the craft of poetry and his often-expressed ambition to rise above common village life inspired long hours of composition and revision. He gradually discarded his other opportunities as he intensified his devotion to the development of his poetic skills.

As he moved into early manhood, however, his interests inevitably broadened. Although he still valued his solitude in nature, his "fondness for study began to decline" as he spent larger amounts of time socializing with fellow laborers.[5] He spent much of his idle time at "Bachelor's Hall," a run-down cottage owned by two brothers, James and John Billings, where the local youth gathered to drink, sing, and tell stories. Later, all but the Billings themselves were to fear the author in their midst because of his power to portray them in his verse, but for a time he moved easily in their company. When away from home, gardening at Burghley Park or burning lime farther afield, he was forced to share the coarser pursuits of fellow workers without the relief he often found in his domestic life at Helpston.

Clare managed to escape much of the rough social life of the agricultural laborer through his relationship with two women. The first, Elizabeth Newbon, produced only a long and stormy courtship; the second, Martha "Patty" Turner, eventually provided a large family and domestic happiness. He first saw Patty crossing a field on her way home and fell in love with her on the spot. Their courtship began when he met her a short time later on his way to a dance at Stamford. He finally overcame the attentions of a rival and the objections of her parents to secure her affections before succumbing to other charms himself. Only Patty's revelation of her pregnancy severed Clare's interest in another girl and brought about his marriage with Patty on March 16, 1820. Although reluctantly married, Clare grew to value Patty's ability to care for his rapidly expanded family and to deal with his own illnesses. After a year of married life he wrote to his publisher of his growing regard for her: "Patt & myself now begin to know each other & live happily & I deem it a fortunate era in my life that I met with her."[6] In the midst of serious illness nine years later he repeated the sentiment almost identically.

Although he wrote several poems to Patty, the real inspiration for his poetry was an earlier, childhood sweetheart, Mary Joyce. Clare met her at the Glinton day school and says he was attracted by her disposition as well as by her physical charm. They spent many hours in each other's company, but Clare seems never to have declared his affection for her except, much later, in his poetry. He was eventually discouraged from contact with her both by his withdrawal from the school and her parents' disapproval of a suitor from the laboring class. Clare continued to hope for a chance to renew their acquaintance, but as the years passed and the possibility of a genuine relationship receded, he began to envisage an intense imaginative relationship, creating out of the real girl either an ideal of true love, a muse, or a guardian spirit, whichever suited his present state of mind and poetic purpose. His attitude to her was complex and constantly shifting, but it developed from a simple regret for a lost opportunity to the grand poetical conception that dominates *Child Harold*. Even from the beginning, however, he seems to have recognized the essentially ideal nature of his feelings toward her. Writing in 1821, for example, he describes their early love as "platonic affection, nothing else but love in idea," and admits that "other Mary's etc., excited my admiration, and the first creator of my warm passions was lost in a perplexed multitude of names."[7] These comments were written not long after his last meeting with the real Mary Joyce and may have been influenced by his recent marriage to Patty, but in any case they reflect his assessment of a real affection for an identifiable woman. He resolved at this point to accept the present reality of his marriage: "I have had the horrors agen upon me by once agen seeing devoted Mary & have written the last doggerel that shall ever sully her name & her remembrance any more tis reflection of the past & not of the present that torments me."[8]

He was not able to keep that resolution. By 1832 he had experienced at least three dreams that featured a female spirit idealized beyond recognition as any living person, but identified by her voice in "The Nightmare" as an embodiment of Mary. In these dreams, one at least of which predates his final meeting with Mary, she appears as prophetess, femme fatale, and guide through the mystery of life. No longer Mary Joyce, she was by this time an entirely symbolic figure. Nine years later, as the chapter on *Child Harold* will demonstrate, she was a complex and not solely ideal figure in his poetry and a confusing personality in his personal life of delusion. Perhaps Clare's most perceptive comment on her significance to him then appears in his letter to Dr. Allen, the keeper of the asylum from which he escaped in July, 1841. There he refers to Patty as "one of my fancys" and to Mary as "my poetical fancy."[9] As early as January, 1821, he had referred to Patty and Mary as his two wives and the delusion intensified in later years, but the distinction between them in the letter to Dr. Allen is an illuminating one. Having escaped from the asylum to return home to Mary, only to find that she had died three years earlier, he was confronted with the final impossibility of uniting his ideal with his real experience. His comments in letters and notes at this time reveal obliquely both his knowledge of, and his refusal to accept this fact. By addressing a letter to her, for instance, he indicates a belief that she is alive, but the letter itself contains veiled admissions that she is no longer physically present: "here I can see Glinton Church & feeling that Mary is safe if not happy I am gratified Though my home is no home to me my hopes are not entirely hopeless while even the memory of Mary lives so near me."[10] The memory remained to inspire poetry in the years to come when he was deprived of even Patty's company; Mary presided over his poetic life as constantly as Patty managed his family and physical well-being.

In 1819 Clare's prospects were bleak: his parents were ill and two years behind in their rent; he was uncertain about his affection for Patty; his accumulation of poems was still known only to himself; and he had not settled on a steady occupation, although the lime burning he was presently engaged in came as close to permanent employment as any he ever had. By the end of 1820, though, he was married, a father, and the author of a book of poetry which had been through four editions. The change in fortune resulted from his encounter with J. B. Henson, a printer at Market Deeping whom Clare had approached about purchasing a notebook for his poems. Having enjoyed a "free application of ale" at the local fair before entering Henson's shop, Clare was less than his usual reluctant self when asked what he required the book for.[11] Henson asked to see a sample of Clare's work, after which he proposed the establishment of a subscription to pay for the printing of a selection. The proposal fell through later when Henson demanded a £15 advance to cover printing costs, but the experience whetted Clare's appetite for publication.

About the same time, he received a demand for payment of a debt he had run up with a bookseller in Stamford. He replied that settlement of the account was impossible but, with a determination lacking in his efforts to gain employment, included samples of his poetry and a suggestion that the bookseller aid him in getting them printed. Although this proprietor scorned the verses, his successor in the business was more impressed. Edward Drury, cousin of John Taylor (the publisher of Keats and Hazlitt), had recently acquired the

Stamford shop and with it Clare's debt. Upon seeing the prospectus, he sought out Clare and asked to see more of his work. Clare's presentation of the poems he had earlier given to Henson initiated a long, sometimes harmonious, often acrimonious relationship between poet and agent. For the moment, however, Clare brought new poems to Drury as he wrote them and Drury looked after Clare's immediate debts and arranged with Taylor to print the poems. *Poems Descriptive of Rural Life and Scenery* appeared on January 16, 1820.

Clare's relationship with Taylor was not always smooth, either, but there can be no doubt that Taylor was instrumental in Clare's immediate success, just as there can be no doubt that Clare was ultimately grateful to him. Taylor introduced Clare's work to the leading journals of the time, the result of which was widespread notice of the book when it appeared. He also edited Clare's future volumes with a diligence that, though not always constant when Taylor's own affairs were in disarray, was always conscientious, and without which the reading public of the day would not have accepted Clare's ill-spelt and unpunctuated work.

The fame that followed publication disconcerted Clare because it brought with it a succession of visitors, many of whom were condescending, patronizing, or simply rude, and all of whom disrupted the quiet home life that he valued. But it also brought the attention of several benefactors who were to help him in later life as well as invitations to visit London, where he met literary men for the first time. He records that he realized the extent of his success as he rode up to London for his initial visit, he in a coach this time while others worked in the fields along the route. He arrived in town just too late to hear one of his own compositions sung by Madame Vestris at Covent Garden, but the following days were filled with marvels that at once delighted and terrified him. In all, he visited London four times, sightseeing, consulting with doctors, making arrangements with his publishers, and attending dinner parties given for his fellow contributors to Taylor's *London Magazine*. Thomas Hood has left a portrait of Clare at one of these dinners:

He was hardy, rough, and clumsy enough to look rustic—like an Ingram's rustic chair. There was a slightness about his frame, with a delicacy of features and complexion, that associated him more with the

Garden than with the Field. . . . There was much about Clare for a
Quaker to like; he was tender-hearted, and averse to violence. How he
recoiled once, bodily-taking his chair along with him,—from a young
surgeon, or surgeon's friend, who let drop, somewhat abruptly, that he
was just come "from seeing a child skinned!"—Clare, from his look of
horror, evidently thought that the poor infant, like Marsyas, had been
flayed alive![12]

Other accounts indicate that Clare was a quiet, but full
participant in these gatherings, even arguing with Charles Lamb
over the admissibility of dialect in poetry. He was, perhaps, more
at home here because of his experience with the Helpston
equivalent, Bachelor's Hall.

The great legacy of these trips was the goodwill he
encountered. For a solitary man lacking in social graces he seems
to have had little trouble forming friendships. He was especially
friendly with E. V. Rippingille, the painter, and Charles Lamb,
both of whom took him to meet other luminaries and to visit
theaters, boxing rings, phrenologists, and other metropolitan
curiosities. Many of these new friends kept up a correspondence
when Clare returned to Helpston, though they little understood
how dependent upon their letters Clare grew for sustaining his
spirits amidst the philistine villagers at home. When they ceased
to write—not always out of indifference, for Clare was not
himself a model correspondent—Clare turned bitter: "the
brotherhood of Poesy has turned out cold indeed but the world is
with them & they forget those who are left in solitude."[13] Later
letters reveal him begging former friends to renew their
correspondence.

In the period covered by these visits, 1820–28, two other
books of his poetry appeared: *The Village Minstrel and Other
Poems* (1821) and *The Shepherd's Calendar* (1827). The period
was marked by fits of prolific composition interspersed with
sometimes lengthy stretches of inactivity caused either by illness
or disillusionment, with the delays in printing *The Shepherd's
Calendar* for example, and by intense conflict between his
private and his poetic lives. Even the natural surroundings of
Helpston could not eliminate his desire for the society and
stimulus of literary friends, and the journeys between Helpston
and London, not to mention his letters, began to reflect this
psychological need.

During this period Clare was gradually forced, in spite of stubborn resistance, to the conclusion that his poetry would never support his growing family and provide the financial independence he sought. Although he continued to experiment in his writing, thus demonstrating his confidence in his poetic powers, he began actively searching for land to establish himself as a farmer. His income at this point consisted essentially of interest earned by investments which had been made on his behalf by benefactors and the very occasional payment for the numerous poems which appeared in literary annuals. This income was not sufficient to support the seven children Patty had borne him by 1832. In that year he finally moved from his native village to a rented cottage with a few acres of land on the Fitzwilliam estate of Lord Milton at Northborough, three miles away. For all the new hopes associated with the move, Clare was reluctant to leave the familiar surroundings of Helpston and the natural environment that was the source and nourishment of his poetry. John Barrell has demonstrated that the move forced Clare to accept, "instead of his earlier notion of the uniqueness of Helpston, a notion of abstract nature."[14] Such a profound change in his relationship with nature was accompanied, as J. W. and Anne Tibble point out, by a further "crisis in his inner life."[15] "The breaking of links with the past," they write, "led him to take stock of the years since 1820, to weigh things up— achievements against mere hopes. He saw himself threatened with pretty total failure."[16]

His sense of failure was relieved momentarily by the mild critical success of the final volume of his verse to appear in his lifetime, *The Rural Muse* (1835). Favorable reviews did not produce sales commensurate with the publicity. However, one of them, in *Druid's Magazine*, contains a rare physical description of Clare at this time and provides an interesting contrast to the earlier glimpse given by Hood:

The first glance at Clare would convince you that he was no common man: he has a forehead of a highly intellectual character; the reflective faculties being exceedingly well developed; but the most striking feature is his eye, light-blue, and flashing with the fire of genius: the peculiar character of his eyes are always remarked by persons when first they see him: his height is rather below the common. His conversation is animated, striking, and full of imagination, yet his dialect is purely provincial.[17]

Whereas the peasant stood out in him for the group of literary men in London, the genius stands out here by contrast with the rustic surroundings that suit his dress and manners. Clare's rapidly changing circumstances are reflected in the attitude of another visitor who described him six years later:

I found him in a field with a hoe or some instrument of the kind, and a pipe in his mouth. He was a small man, not stout, and yet of a frame sufficiently muscular, a fresh complexion, high forehead, a nose approaching the aquiline, and a long, full chin. His countenance was pleasing, but as it struck me, not remarkably intellectual, still less betokening one endowed with the rare poetical talents with which nature had gifted him. . . . I observed in Clare no aberration of mind for some time. Only once, without any connection with such a subject, he broke out into a mention of prize fighting, but it was abruptly, as if it had struck him suddenly, and wholly, so far as I could judge, without any association of ideas excited by what was near him, any more than as connected with the subject of our conversation. It was like breaking out of an interloping thought into language owing to some accidental prompting while a different subject was under discussion. I observed no other appearance of mental derangement.[18]

Hood had expected, and found, a rustic; the reviewer in 1835 had expected, and found, a genius; Cyrus Redding, the writer here, expected a lunatic and found only a gentle man working in the fields.

But he did notice signs of the affliction that had brought Clare to the asylum at High Beech, Essex, four years earlier. The move to High Beech was the culmination of years of sporadic illness, both physical and, in the forms of occasional depression or anxiety, mental. From his youth he had suffered epileptiform fits, and in later life was plagued by severe stomach pains, numbness in parts of his body, a "prickly feel about the face & temples,"[19] and other disorders. The extent of his mental illness in 1836–37 is still not clear, but it was sufficient to drive John Taylor to visit Clare, accompanied by a physician, in December of 1836. Shortly thereafter Taylor met Dr. Matthew Allen, was impressed by his new techniques for mental treatment, and arranged to have Clare placed under Allen's supervision. At High Beech Clare experienced a measure of tranquility, working in the fields, as Redding noted, and enjoying the freedom to rove through the grounds and to write poetry. That poetry, however, especially *Don Juan*, reveals the inner turmoil that his outward appearance and conduct belied. In private he resented being separated from his family and was confused by his enforced companionship with people who were obviously mad.

Shortly after Redding's visit a gypsy pointed out to Clare a possible route of escape from the asylum. Given the low priority that Allen placed on security, the method outlined by the gypsy was less important than the suggestion that escape was one of Clare's options. On July 20, 1841, Clare walked out of the asylum grounds and continued walking for four days, with nothing more to eat than a plug of chewing tobacco and the grass he found along the way, until he reached home. He was allowed to remain there under Patty's care, writing and revising parts of *Child Harold* and wandering the fens, for the next five months. When it became clear that he could not remain at home he was examined by two doctors who pronounced him insane. He was taken to the Northampton General Lunatic Asylum on December 29, 1841.

His years at Northampton were similar to those at High Beech. He was allowed the freedom of the grounds and given permission to go into town where he spent hours sitting under the portico of All Saints' Church watching the crowds pass and occasionally conversing with the townspeople for whom he frequently scribbled verses on envelopes or other scraps of paper. His delusions multiplied, however, and the accounts of contemporary visitors record his increasing retreat into personal fantasies, though he never approached absolute madness. From 1845 to 1850 his sense of despair was at least partially alleviated by the interest taken in his poetry by the steward during these years, W. F. Knight. Knight transcribed all of Clare's verses that he could find and encouraged him to write others. As a result, many that would otherwise have vanished and some that might not have been written at all have been preserved.

Several letters to his children and Patty survive to give some insight into his life at Northampton—they demonstrate a confused and deteriorating mind. After 1854 he was confined to the asylum grounds, his estrangement from the outside world and his family growing even more complete. He was visited occasionally by his children, never by his wife. He died on May 20, 1864, ten days after suffering a paralytic seizure. Although his constantly expressed wish to die at home was denied him by the circumstances of his life, his body was transported back to Helpston for burial in the churchyard.

CHAPTER 2

The Poetic Eye

I Clare and Wordsworth

PERHAPS overly impressed with the lyrical purity of his later songs or the unique descriptive style of his nature poems, with his apparently simple love for natural beauty or his consuming passion for an idealized woman, Clare's readers have been reluctant to appreciate as a thinker the man they originally discovered as a "peasant poet." Since the contemporary reviews of his first volume, the most persistent charge against Clare has been that his descriptions are vivid and accurate, but his poems lack the element of thought that characterizes the nature poetry of his contemporaries. Comparisons with Wordsworth abound, stressing the "principle of inward growth" and the "range of his imaginative apprehension,"[1] or the psychological interest "in the workings of the mind"[2] to ostensibly distinguish the great poetry of Wordsworth from the merely good poetry of Clare. But they fail in the end to advance our appreciation of either poet. John Middleton Murry's contention that Clare demonstrated "nothing of the principle of inward growth, which gives to Wordsworth's most careless work a place within the unity of a great scheme"[3] and his more damaging, though not unrelated, claim that "Clare could not, while Wordsworth could, think long and deeply,"[4] undermine the other, often complimentary remarks he makes about Clare. When this assessment was made, of course, most of Wordsworth's thoughts on the subject of poetry were publicly available, whereas Clare's views were confined to the few poems, and almost no prose, that had been published at that time. Subsequent revelations of Clare's thoughts, some published, others still in manuscript, easily refute Murry's charge by revealing Clare's intelligent and sensitive mind.

In many of these sources Clare assesses his own capacity for thought. In one of the numerous prose fragments scattered throughout his manuscripts, he subordinates his indisputable sensory pleasure in contact with nature to the mental exercise he found necessary to enhance such experiences:

Pleasures are of two kinds—one arises from cultivation of the mind & is enjoyed only by the few—& this is the most lasting & least liable to change—the more common pleasures are found by the many like beautiful weeds in a wilderness they are of natural growth & though very beautiful to the eye are only annuals—these may be called the pleasures of the passions & belong only to the different stages of our existence.[5]

He anticipated attacks on his intellectual ability by reminding us in his autobiography of the difference between education and intelligence:

As to my learning I am not wonderfully deep in science nor so wonderfully ignorant as many have fancied I puzzled over everything in my hours of leisure with a restless curiosity that was ever on the enquiry & never satisfied when I got set fast in one thing I did not tire but tried at another tho with the same success in the end yet it never sickend me I still pursued knowledge in a new path & tho I never came off victorious I was never conquered.[6]

The persistence he mentions here is continually demonstrated by the restless mental activity he revealed in his prose and verse, and its success not only by the penetrating insights in many of his poems, but by the skill with which he conveys these insights, without overt intellectualization, in his best poems. And the humility and curiosity demonstrated in this passage are evident in his attempts to formulate a theory of poetry based on his own experiences of composition. He was an intelligent and perceptive man. He thought often and deeply about the phenomenon of creating poetry out of his sensitive responses to nature; his dedication to the muse excited him early and sustained him through the darkest times of his life.

The comparison with Wordsworth need not stress an absence of thought in Clare so much as a compatibility of thought between him and his great contemporary. Clare, after all, admired Wordsworth more than any other poet of the time, even Byron. "I read Wordsworth oftener," he confessed to a visitor in

1825, "than I did Byron."[7] Although he was often impatient with Wordsworth's "affected Godliness" and "mysteries," he included him in "a list of favourite Poems and Poets who went to nature for their images."[8] Perhaps his admiration was accented by the prejudice he had to overcome before reading the older poet in the first place: "When I first began to read poetry I dislikd Wordsworth because I heard he was dislikd & I was astonishd when I lookd into him to find my mistaken pleasure in being delighted & finding him so natural and beautiful."[9] As Clare's critical independence developed, his admiration intensified into love. In a sonnet given to Cyrus Redding when he visited Clare in 1841, Clare frankly admits:

> Wordsworth I love; his books are like the fields,
> Not filled with flowers, but works of human kind.[10]

But the parallels between the two poets must be drawn with caution. Too many critics, like Harold Bloom, have dismissed Clare's thoughts on poetry as mere shadows of Wordsworth's theories.[11] A similar attitude leads Geoffrey Grigson to call "Pastoral Poesy," one of Clare's major statements on poetic composition, a "curious extract of Wordsworth, Coleridge, and Clare,"[12] thereby implying some direct debt on Clare's part. And Mark Storey calls the same poem "a rather curious amalgamation of ideas culled from his reading of Coleridge and Wordsworth."[13] Both passages leave the impression that Clare systematically analyzed Wordsworth's and Coleridge's writings, as many modern critics have done, to extract a theory of poetry, then adapted that theory to his own method of composition. Quite apart from the fact that we have no evidence Clare read all the material available at the time, we do know that a major portion of Wordsworth's theory, as correlated by M. H. Abrams, W. J. B. Owen, James Heffernan, and others, was not available to him. Wordsworth's letters and much of his prose, not to mention his most ambitious poetic statement, *The Prelude*, were not published until long after Clare's own thoughts on his art had emerged. A more likely source for the fundamental conformity between some of the two poets' views of their art is the similarity of the method by which they perceived natural objects and landscapes, a method which Clare adopted as a sensitive boy raised in close proximity to nature and which he began to develop even in his earliest poetry. Clare did not need another poet to teach him how to respond to nature, nor did he benefit much from other poets' theories in writing his own poems. That poetry grew, as much for Clare as for Wordsworth, out of his personal ramblings in nature. The resemblances in theory, (couched for the most part in radically different language), support the authenticity of the process they were both describing. The culmination of eighteenth-century poetics, as of eighteenth-century philosophy, was a method based on observation of experience rather than citation of authorities. Wordsworth and Clare, in relative isolation, came to similar conclusions from observations of their individual minds at work in the composition of poetry.

II   *The Poet's Mind*

Clare deserves his reputation for striking and detailed descriptions of natural objects, but such description was not the end he strove for; he sought a means of communicating his special vision of the natural world. Although he maintained that his art consisted primarily of recording what he saw or felt in the presence of nature, he also noticed a difference between what he perceived and what was perceptible to those who lacked a poet's sensitivity. This attitude accounts for his apparently simple explanation of perception in "Sighing for Retirement," where he contends:

> I found the poems in the fields,
> And only wrote them down.[14]

As we will see, a poem is wrought, for Clare, by bringing the special powers of a poet's mind to bear on the raw material it finds in nature. This view considers the poet a collector and recorder of perceptions, of artifacts which appear to him complete at the moment he finds them, rather than a creator who invents and arranges new images into works of art. Clare deplored much of the artifice he saw in the poetry around him because it interfered with the direct communication from the natural world, through the poet, to the reader. Keats, a poet he otherwise admired, was guilty of this kind of unfaithfulness:

His descriptions of scenery are often very fine but as it is the case with other inhabitants of great cities he often described nature as she appeared to his fancies & not as he would have described her had he witnessed the things he describes—Thus it is he has often undergone the stigma of Cockneyism & what appears as beautys in the eyes of a pent-up citizen are looked upon as consciets by those who live in the country.[15]

Keats's subsequent success has somewhat overshadowed Clare's criticism, but the principle expounded here is the basis for Clare's own most successful work.

It reveals how firmly Clare felt the necessity of accurately transcribing natural images. One of his most persistent themes is artistic integrity, an integrity which he often gauged by a poet's fidelity to the natural image. He distrusted those who moved away from what was perceived in nature:

Art may ply fantastic anatomy but nature is always herself in her wildest moods of extravagance—Arts penalty is a beautiful vagary a vision a romance—& like the moral pictures of nature in books we look about us & cannot find anything like them elsewhere.[16]

In order to emphasize the primacy of natural imagery he redefined Pope's famous dictum regarding truth to nature in his own terms:

> A pleasing image to its page conferred
> In living character and breathing word
> Becomes a landscape heard and felt and seen
> Sunshine and shade one harmonizing green
> Where meads and brooks and forrests basking lie
> Lasting as truth and the eternal sky
> Thus truth to nature as the true sublime
> Stands a mount atlas overpeering time.[17]

The poet's power arises from his ability to transfer a natural image from the material world into a verbal equivalent on the page. Clare's desire to achieve this faithful correspondence between the original landscape and the literary one became the touchstone for his critiques of other poets. He scorned those who allowed a consciousness of their audience to interfere with their vision of the natural world:

While some affectations are striving for a life-time to hit all tastes, by only writing as they fancy all feel, and by not trusting to their own feelings, miss the mark by a wide throw, an unconscious poet of little name writes a trifle as he feels, without thinking of others, or fancying that he feels it, and becomes a common name. Unaffected simplicity is the everyday picture of nature.[18]

Such a simplicity of response breathes through Clare's own poetry and forms the foundation of his poetic theory.

Clare seldom drew his images from any source other than nature. Since images project more than verbal meaning, he felt that they, more than the words used to describe them, contained the essence of poetry: "True poesy is not in words / But images that thoughts express."[19] As the Tibbles have pointed out, Clare's poetry often relies on the image rather than the word, the picture rather than the syntactical formality of the discourse. "Clare was not," they feel, "interested in words as words; nor did he pay much attention to their formal grouping into sentences. The unit for him was the short phrase or clause—the verbal expression of the image upon which his attention was focused."[20] This distinction is useful if we do not lose sight of Clare's intense interest in dialect and in the right word or phrase to capture his image. He was interested in words insofar as they were his only means of conveying what he saw, but the real art, for Clare, lay in the quality of perception which transcends mere verbal description, that could be conveyed only through thoughts requiring more than the individual word for their effect.

To transcribe natural images accurately required more than simply holding the mirror to nature. Clare's experience provides further support for M. H. Abram's warning against taking the mirror analogue too literally.[21] Clare found that to "look on nature with a poetic eye magnifies the pleasure she herself being the very essence & soul of Poesy."[22] A lens, rather than a mirror, intensified the joy Clare felt when perceiving natural images, giving to the image itself the aura of wonder which pervades most of his nature poetry. This alteration revealed to Clare's especially sensitive mind not simply a bird, but a hermit; not a snowdrop, but a "lovely woman"—in short, not an object but a corresponding image which transformed the original object into a source of greater joy.[23]

This lens was the poet's mind. Like Wordsworth, Clare was

aware that he perceived nature with a sensitivity not common to all men. In his attempts to explain the mental faculty that enabled him to do so, he differed from Wordsworth in details— and especially in vocabulary—but he agreed that some men were better equipped to perceive objects in an aesthetic way. The distinguishing faculty he called "taste," a term which no doubt occurred to him from his reading of eighteenth-century poetry, but which he adapted for his own purposes to designate what Wordsworth would have called a "lively sensibility":

> In every trifle somthing lives to please
> Or to instruct us—every weed or flower
> Heirs beauty as a birthright by degrees
> Of more or less though taste alone hath power
> To see and value what the herd pass bye.[24]

As this passage suggests, taste for Clare was the capacity to perceive and appreciate the beauty inherent in natural objects. It enabled him to "look on nature with a poetic feeling."[25]

In this sense Clare is clearly departing from previous meanings of the word "taste." The much-discussed history of the word in the century preceding Clare's use of it considered it primarily as a term of literary criticism. It denoted the critic's power of discrimination as applied to works of art rather than to objects in nature. In spite of Ralph Cohen's contention that the "term taste began to lose all specific reference" after 1750,[26] R. L. Brett manages to detect a shift in its dominant meaning from a form of judgment in the earlier eighteenth century toward a "sense," or an intuitive ability to detect beauty in art, later.[27] He also notices that eighteenth-century critics using the term tend more and more to see the critic's function as a vicariously artistic one. A good critic, according to both Dennis and Farquar, is one who can, in Brett's words, "enter into the creative processes of the poet's mind."[28] Unconcerned with, at times even scornful of, criticism, Clare extended the word to describe the poet's own facility to grasp intuitively the inherent beauty of his environment when he confronted it. Wordsworth, on the other hand, invested "taste" with no meaning beyond its general significance of discretion in criticism.

The extent to which Clare diverges from tradition in his use of "taste" is evident in one of his early sonnets:

- - - - - - - Taste is from heaven
A inspiration nature cant bestow
Tho natures beautys where a taste is given
Warms the ideas of the soul to flow
With that enchanting 'thusiastic glow
That throbs the bosom when the curious eye
Glances on beautious things that give delight
Objects of earth or air or sea or sky
That bring the very senses in the sight
To relish what it sees—but all is night
To the gross clown—natures unfolded book
As on he blunders never strikes his eye
Pages of landscape tree and flower and brook
Like bare blank leaves he turns unheeded bye.[29]

Something of what Clare means is immediately obvious: taste is not inherent in nature, nor is it simply a cultured response to art. It is a faculty of the poet's mind which reacts with natural objects to form a chain of ideas which eventually produces a feeling of intense love for those objects. As a type of inspiration it is inexplicable, but also productive of art; it initiates a process through which the poet experiences an escalating sense of pleasure in what begins as mere physical perception. The stages of gradual excitement in this experience are recreated in the verse itself. The initially fluid lines give way to metrical agitation in lines four and five, thereby suggesting the progressive excitement of the sensitive mind. The periodic structure and the compelling metrical movement of the long clause through lines six to ten reinforce the process of the mind embracing the multifarious scene and gradually rendering it into a sensation of pleasure. This movement of verse is immediately contrasted by the relatively awkward qualifying phrases used to describe the rustic clown's blundering reaction to the potentially enlightening scene in the final lines.

Clare defines taste, then, as an innate gift which enables certain people to respond with intense emotion to natural beauty. That it is a latent quality is clear from its inability to produce enthusiasm independently of natural objects, although it enables these objects themselves to "warm the ideas of the soul to flow / with [an] enchanting 'thusiastic glow." It is normally quiescent becoming active only when inspired, or triggered, by natural objects. Since it only reacts to some objects, those which possess distinctive qualities identifying them as one of nature's "beauties," it is a selective agent. In "The Bramble," for example, taste "marks" the "scorn wronged bush" as "worthy praise."[30] Elsewhere, too, Clare emphasizes this function of selectivity: taste "modif[ies] expression & selects images it arranges & orders matters & thoughts."[31] This fragmentary comment is at best ambiguous, but taken in the context of his belief that poetry resides in "images that thoughts express,"[32] it seems to suggest that that part of the mind which he designates "taste" selects and arranges the images. Once it has selected these images, taste "endears"[33] them to the poet so that he appreciates ("relishes") what he sees. Clare describes this power in "Shadows of Taste," where he sees it transforming the landscape:

> Minds spring as various as the leaves of trees
> To follow taste and all her sweets explore
> And Edens make where deserts spread before.[34]

By this method taste "hath power / to see and value what the herd pass bye."[35] Although he does not always identify taste as the distinguishing feature of his mind, as he does in "On Taste," Clare seems always aware of the distance it marked between his mind and that of the average man:

> I could not walk the fields like common men
> And have no fancys nourish—nor could I
> Pass the wild rose bush oer the foxes den
> And not admire its grandeur silently.[36]

He describes this same reaction in "Shadows of Taste," but there identifies taste as the mental quality that enables even some scientists to respond aesthetically:

> But he the man of science and of taste
> Sees wealth far richer in the worthless waste
> Where bits of lichen and a sprig of moss
> Will all the rapture of his mind engross
> And bright winged insects on the flowers of may
> Shine pearls too wealthy to be cast away.[37]

He considered taste to be an attribute of a universal wisdom shared by animals, birds, and flowers as well as men. Thus a moorhen's wisdom in choosing the safest, most ideal spot for its nest is based on "the taste / they have to choose such homes upon the waste / rich architects," a taste which finds "picturesque" settings rather than simply functional ones.[38] So also in "Shadows of Taste," after reiterating that all natural creatures, including flowers which possess "the wisdom of creative choice," share in varying degrees this quality of mind, Clare relates it to wisdom:

> Such are the various moods that taste displays
> Surrounding wisdom in concentring rays
> Where threads of light from one bright focus run
> As days proud halo circles round the sun.[39]

He has defined taste earlier in the poem as "the instinctive mood" with which creatures "choose for joy" their natural habitat. This passage establishes a metaphoric hierarchy based on the proximity of the individual's taste to a central, though undefined, concept of wisdom. The poet's preeminent rank in this hierarchy becomes clear from another passage in the same poem:

> And man that noble insect restless man
> Whose thoughts scale heaven in its mighty span
> Pours forth his living soul in many a shade
> And taste runs riot in her every grade
> While the low herd mere savages subdued
> With nought of feeling or of taste imbued
> Pass over sweetest scenes a careless eye
> As blank as midnight in its deepest dye.

We could be forgiven for mistaking this use of the word for its eighteenth-century sense, if it were not for the context. But here the man who lacks taste also lacks the impulse to "pour forth his living soul" when in contact with nature; the man of taste rises above ignorance to a poet's relationship with nature.

A second mental peculiarity of the poet that alters his perception of natural objects Clare called "genius." Although he often used that term to denote nothing more than superior intelligence, in several of his comments on poetic composition he reserves for it a more technical meaning. In "Dawning of Genius," for example, he defines it as "a pleasing rapture of the mind / a kindling warmth to Learning unconfin'd."[40] Whereas he considered taste to be a latent desire for the appreciation of beauty which selects images for the poet's consideration, he saw genius as a faculty which acts upon the perceived images in a state of mental excitement, or "rapture." Taste applies to the initial perception, genius to the ensuing mental reaction to it. The remainder of "Dawning of Genius" gives a more detailed account of the effects of this faculty:

> Genius a pleasing rapture of the mind
> A kindling warmth to learning unconfin'd
> Glows in each breast and flutters every vein
> From arts Refinements to th' unculter'd swain
> Such is that warmth the lowly shepherd proves
> Pacing his native fields and willow Groves
> Such is that joy which every scene unfolds
> Which taste endeareth and fond memory holds
> Such is that sympathy his heart attends
> Makes bush and tree companions seem and friends
> Such is that fondness from his soul sincere
> That makes his native place so doubly dear.

Genius is active: it kindles, glows, and flutters. It is identified with warmth, joy, sympathy, and fondness, indicating it is an attitude that reacts to the images "endeared" to it by taste. If it is not quite Coleridge's "colouring of the imagination," it is at least a force that transforms the ordinary into the valued through a process of mental excitement. And Clare's consistent use of the imagery of ignition—he even refers to "sparks of genius" in another line of the poem—itself reveals the burst of emotional insight he embodied in the term. Elsewhere in this poem the enthusiastic transformation of the scene is expressed through the same imagery when Clare describes the effect of genius working in a ploughman's mind:

> Raptures the while his inward powers inflame
> And Joys delight him which he cannot name.

The influence of taste, although not here designated, attracts the mind to its surroundings even to the point of his actively "picking" the stone and shell, while the rapture of genius transforms them into a source of transcendent joy. As genius "dawns," it intensifies the experience as "increasing beauties fresh'ning on his sight / unfold new charms and witness more delight." The result is an inexplicable sense of joy:

> He feels enraptur'd tho' he knows not why
> And turns and mutters o'er his joys in vain
> And dwells on something which he can't explain.

A transitory glimpse of insight follows: "the bursts of thought with which his souls perplexd / are bred one moment and are gone the next." Time and again, in Clare's poems as in his theory, the experience leads to a frustrating realization of the inadequacy of language to express the intensity of his perception:

> Ideas picture pleasing views to mind
> For which his language can no utterance find.

What remains of this intense experience are occasionally recurring glimpses of memory which are related to the original pleasure as sparks are to a dying coal. He extends the metaphor of ignition to describe the remnant of his ecstatic moment:

> Yet still the heart will kindling sparks retain
> And thoughts will rise and fancy strive again
> (So have I markt the dying embers light
> When on the hearth it fainted from my sight
> A glimmering glow oft redens up again
> And sparks crack bright'ning into light in vain)
> Still lingering out its kindling hopes to rise
> Till faint and fainter the last twinkle dies.

The process described here is further evidence of Clare's difference from Wordsworth. He finds no virtue in "emotion recollected in tranquility" and the imagery he uses to describe the process is particularly individual, expressing what he felt happening in his moments of poetic response to nature rather than a variation on the theme of another poet.

Genius, then, is another attribute of the poetic mind which, independently of education or intellectual refinement, enables the poet to respond to the aesthetic elements of nature. It produces out of the raw material provided by taste, "that joy which every scene unfolds / which taste endeareth and fond memory holds." These two elements of the mind are responsible for the alteration of the natural image. One is by definition selective, therefore altering through exclusion of unwanted details; the other is highly emotional, therefore distorting by the subjectivity of its response. Combined, they provide the poet with a capacity to perceive nature poetically.

III Self-Creating Joy

The prerequisite for initiating the mental activity that produced poetry, Clare felt, was an environment of complete isolation and relative silence in which a reciprocal communication with nature was possible. The reverence he held for solitude he summed up in his admission that "solitude and God are one,"[41] and the effect that it had on his mind he acknowledged in "To the Snipe":

> From dangers reach
> Here thou art safe to roam
> Far as these washy flag grown marshes stretch
> A still and quiet home
>
> In these thy haunts
> Ive gleaned habitual love
> From the vague world where pride and folly taunts
> I muse and look above
>
> Thy solitudes
> The unbounded heaven esteems
> And here my heart warms into higher moods
> And dignifying dreams.[42]

Solitude with nature, here, initiates an escalating process of response which culminates in the poet extracting, or gleaning, a new state of mind which, because he suggests it is habitual, has become a permanent part of his experience. In another poem this gentle pleasure arising from solitude is replaced by a more forceful response: "A mind oerflowing with excess / of joys that spring from solitude."[43] Clare responded to silence; it was more to him than simple absence of sound. Thus his desire for solitude was based on the prospect, always a pleasant one for him, of silent communication, "for Nature's voice is never loud; I seek

for quiet joys."[44] Throughout his career he reiterated his belief
that "silence speaks."[45]

As the passage to the snipe indicates, Clare found that silent
meditation awakened his mind to poetic activity by warming his
heart into higher moods. His contemplation of nature was seldom
relaxing because his mind responded to the stimuli of silence in
much the same way Coleridge's does in "Frost at Midnight." His
awakening was impulsive, beyond his own powers to arrest, as he
indicates in "A Lair at Noon":

> I fain had slept but flies would buzz around
> I fain had looked calmly on the scene
> But the sweet snug retreat my search had found
> Wakend the muse to sing the willow screne.[46]

This awakening is the first mental act of Clare's poetic process.
Since it precedes the act of composing it is not necessarily
mentioned in the poem itself, but it is described in several poems
which record various stages of the process. It is described
through another metaphor of ignition, for example, in "The
Village Minstrel":

> Nature lookd on him wi a witching eye
> Her pleasing scenes were his delightful book
> Where he. . . wi wild enthusiasm us'd to look. . .
> And fir'd wi what he saw hum oer some simple song.[47]

More often this instantaneous impulse is replaced by a gradual
process of "warming," as it is in the passage from "To the Snipe,"
or in another from "Winter Rainbow":

> And what wild eye wi natures beauties charmd
> That hangs enrapturd oer each witching spell
> Can see thee winter then and not be warmd
> To breath thy praise and say "I love thee well."[48]

In either case the impulse to express his pleasure, or pain in other
poems, arises while he meditates on nature in a state of isolation
and silence.

Clare is much less specific about the second stage of this poetic
process, the transfer of selected images to the mind. He does
indicate that it is an automatic, inexplicable movement from the

landscape to a meditative mind, when he acknowledges in "Sunset Visions" that, simply, "something cometh to the gazing mind."[49] And in the context of his statement in "Pastoral Poesy" that true poetry consists "not in words, but images," his later comment in that poem that "an image to the mind is brought" implies a similar view of this transference. The movement is from external to internal, from concrete object to abstract thought, a movement which he illustrates in the same poem:

> But poesy is a language meet
> And fields are everyones employ
> The wild flower neath the shepherds feet
> Looks up and gives him joy
>
> A language that is ever green
> That feelings unto all impart
> As awthorn blossoms soon as seen
> Give may to every heart.[50]

The movement from natural object (blossoms) to thought (concept of beauty associated with May) provides the mind with the material for expression in poetry. Thus, almost literally, "the wild flower 'neath the shepherd's feet / looks up and gives him joy." The image does not give itself back to the sensitive eye; it gives a sensation of joy. In "Dawning of Genius" Clare transforms the noun "picture" into a verb to give something of the quality of instantaneous transformation he finds in this moment of imaginative perception: "ideas picture pleasing views to mind."[51] The ideas which come to the mind bring with them the view that inspired them, the two coalesce into a joy "which he cannot name."

While Clare believed that anyone with a poet's mind—not only writers, since illiterate shepherds and ploughmen are constantly looking on nature with a "poetic eye" in his verse— could experience this special insight, he also felt that their heightened perception depended on that mind being in a particularly receptive state. Because

> An image to the mind is brought
> Where happiness enjoys
> An easy thoughtlessness of thought
> And meets excess of joys.[52]

This suggests the image is transferred to a mind that is engaged in an unselfconscious, or unself-analyzing, intellectual activity. It implies there must be thoughts, but that they must not be thoughts *of* thoughts. The mental activity must be directed out toward the external object rather than back into its own locus of mentation. Clare was saying the same thing when he stressed the unconscious aspects of the honest poet in his essay on "Popularity in Authorship," quoted earlier in this chapter. And he reiterated it later in life in *Child Harold:*

> And he who studies natures volume through
> And reads it with a pure unselfish mind
> Will find Gods power all round in every view
> As one bright vision of the almighty mind.[53]

Purity and unselfishness presuppose a receptive mind which does not attempt to manipulate what it sees. Such a mind produces revelations of what Wordsworth would call "the life of things." In Clare's scheme this lack of self-consciousness allows the operation of the "inward powers" of genius on images supplied by the selective element of taste.

The natural propensity of the mind in this state is to attempt to preserve the image presented to it. Thus when viewing a landscape in his sonnet "Written in Autumn," Clare attempts to freeze the scene even though it appeals to him by its transitoriness. This paradox he expresses in his desire for autumn to "lastingly decline."[54] Elsewhere he describes this attempt more fully:

> I gazd upon them wi' a wishing eye
> And longd but vainly for the painters power
> To give existance to the mingling dye
> And snatch a beauty from an evening hour.[55]

Again the significant characteristic of the scene is its transitoriness, and again the poet wishes to make it static by giving it "existence" and by snatching its beauty out of the progression of change in which it is involved. In Clare's realization of the futility of such an attempt, coupled with his desire to continue it, lies the poignancy of this poetic experience. He continues:

But soft and soft it lost its self in night
And changd and changd in many a lumind track
I felt concernd to see it leave the sight
And hide its lovley face in blanking black.

In this case the poem itself is an attempt to trace the gradual change and eventual disappearance of the cloud and becomes therefore more effective than even the painter at capturing the essential transitory quality of the scene. The wistful mood and simple personification combine with the repetition of "soft" and "changd" to convey an impression of the progress of the sunset, an impression made possible only by the time span required to read the poem. But in spite of this advantage of the poet's, Clare continued to feel, in the midst of the poetic experience, a desire to capture the momentary beauty which he could feel passing by.

He translated this desire into his own concept of poetic form. After completing *The Shepherd's Calendar,* itself a series of pictures and stories from rural life, he outlined to his publisher, John Taylor, a plan to compose a particular style of sonnet: "I have made it up in my mind to write one hundred Sonnets as a set of pictures on the scenes of objects that appear in the different seasons."[56] In practice these sonnets turn out to contain not only pictures and objects, but a fluidity and motion in their description that often stresses their place in the continuum from which he has wrested them. Ian Jack noticed the tendency to create composed pictures in the sonnets: "as we turn over his hundreds of sonnets we become aware that he was experimenting endlessly to find a verbal equivalent for the small woodcut so brilliantly practiced by Bewick."[57] But Edmund Blunden came closer to the point when he praised the sonnets because he saw the transitory nature of the experience contained in them: "his finest work in his contemporary volumes of verse . . . is contained in sonnets and other brief pieces conveying . . . momentary impressions of nature with startling power."[58] Clare recognized in the poetic process a natural tendency of mind to capture the fleeting image, and this tendency was revealed in the form his poetry took, not only in the sonnets and shorter lyrics, but also in the succession of individual scenes which constitute many of his longer poems. Indeed, he acknowledged it as part of his personal method of perception:

And then I walk and swing my stick for joy
And catch at little pictures passing bye
A gate whose posts are two old dotterel trees
A close with molehills sprinkled oer its leas
A little footbrig with its crossing rail
A wood gap stopt with ivy wreathing pale.[59]

The diction in the second line of this passage is particularly revealing because it depicts two, not unrelated, types of poem that resulted from his method. On the surface he appears to be describing a type in which he records his own movement through the landscape, extracting as he goes scenes which he molds into the progression of the poem. But the ambivalence of "pictures passing bye" suggests another type, too, in which the scenes themselves are passing, in time, through his imagination as he views the landscape. His purpose is to capture individual scenes before they are lost. Both kinds of poem confirm his belief in the image as a primary component of both nature and poetry.

But the image he tries to preserve is not merely a tree or a stream, or even an interesting amalgam of natural objects. He does not consider the natural object perceived by the sensitive mind as simply a material, so much as a fusion of material and literary image—a metaphor or a symbol. In its ability to appreciate this fusion, the poetic mind is unique. After discussing the transference of images to the mind in "Pastoral Poesy," Clare gives an example of the difference between minds that fuse and those that remain ignorant of poetic perception:

The storm from which the shepherd turns
To pull his beaver down
While he upon the heath sojourns
Which autumn bleaches brown

Is music aye and more indeed
To those of musing mind
Who through the yellow woods proceed
And listen to the wind

The poet in his fitful glee
And fancys many moods
Meets it as some strange melody
And poem of the woods . . .

> And now a harp that flings around
> The music of the wind
> The poet often hears the sound
> When beauty fills the mind . . .
>
> So would I my own mind employ
> And my own heart impress
> That poesy's self's a dwelling joy
> Of humble quietness.[60]

Whereas the shepherd, self-conscious and aware only of the threatening aspect of the storm (because his mind is inward-oriented), sees it simply as an element from which to seek shelter, the poet, being in a state of "easy thoughtlessness of thought" and listening to the wind (i.e., being outward-oriented), sees it as a "poem of the woods"—the kind of poem Clare claims to have found in the fields and written down. Since he sees the storm through the faculties of taste and genius he sees not merely a physical spectacle of accumulating dark clouds and increasing wind velocity, but rather a fusion of these elements with the metaphor of an imaginary harp and its music. From a passive, musing state through a period of ecstasy, "in his fitful glee / and fancys many moods," which makes it possible for him to appreciate the "strange melody" and "music of the wind," he progresses to a desire for further mental activity in the last stanza quoted. What is important here is his mode of perception; he describes only what he sees, but he is conscious of seeing in a unique way—he finds metaphors where the shepherd finds only physical phenomena.

This transforming power of the poet's mind is repeatedly stressed in his poetry, especially in those poems that describe some aspect of the poetic process. In "Poesy," for instance, his state of mind makes natural objects appear as companions who "tell their tales of joy and grief and think and feel as me."[61] Speaking to the muse which he calls "Poesy" in "The Moorehens Nest," he praises her power to lift his mind at least temporarily out of "this rude world its trouble and its care" into the realm of imaginative fusion of both worlds:

> I pick up flowers and pebbles and by thee
> As gems and jewels they appear to me
> I pick out pictures round the fields that lie

> In my minds heart like things that cannot die
> Like picking hopes and making friends with all.[62]

Both individual objects and complete scenes are transformed
into metaphors which enhance his pleasure in regarding the
originals. He is describing not so much the mind's facility to make
natural objects stand as metaphors for something else—an ability
he also demonstrates in his work—as he is the mind's propensity
to bring other concepts to bear on the perception of natural
objects so that the original is perceived with greater insight. He
also explains, here, the transitory nature of his glimpses of this
fusion:

> Yet glass will often bear a harder fall
> As bursting bottles loose the precious wine
> Hopes casket breaks and I the gems resign.

But in the brief moment of poetic perception he has added the
concept of gems and jewels to flowers and pebbles, in much the
same way he sees "patriarchs" which "wear an ancient passion"
in "The Robin's Nest,"[63] whereas the ordinary mind would only
see weeds.

Clare never does make it clear at what point in the poetic
process the object adopts the qualities of metaphor or symbol,
but his statement that it occurs to one in "fitful glee" and "fancys
many moods" would suggest that the transformation occurs in
conjunction with the mental excitement of genius, a suggestion
supported by his claim that "taste is a uniformity of excellence it
modif[ies] expression and selects images it aranges and orders
matters and thoughts but genius creates them."[64] The creative
function of genius distinguishes it from the rather mechanical
proclivity of taste. Creation of thoughts suggests the active
fusion of the real object and the imagined one into the concept of
joy which invariably results. In "The Moorehen's Nest" he
records the progress of the excitement which forges these
concepts as "loading the heart with joys it cannot bear / that
warms and chills and burns and bursts at last,"[65] and in
"Expression" he calls it the "muses fire," describing its method as

> Stealing the music of some angels song
> To tell of all he sees and all admires
> Which fancys colours paint so sweet so strong![66]

Although the language of these excerpts is more fanciful than definitive, it does convey the intensity of feeling which Clare associated with the climax of the poetic process.

IV *The Poem*

The eventual result of this mental activity is what Clare calls the "throbbing utterance of the soul,"[67] the work of art. His exalted state of mind produces a desire to express the quality of his immediate experience:

> The very winds sing sonnets to the sky
> And sunshine bids them welcome—so that I
> Feel a new being as from healthier climes
> And shape my idle fancys into ryhmes
> Of natures extacy in bursting flowers.[68]

With characteristic humility Clare credits nature with the real creative power, but his apparently naïve comment is only a reiteration of his special concept of the poet as transcriber. As we have seen, the poet's mind interacts with nature to produce both the ecstasy and the rhymes. The ideal product of this interaction is a work of art which has grown out of, and gained its character from, the original experience:

real excellence must be its own creation it must be the overflowings of its own mind & must *make* its admirers willing converts from its own powerful consceptions & not yield to win them by giving way to their opinions of excellence which turns out in time to be nothing more than mere importers of fashions mysterys of pretensions.[69]

The echoes of Wordsworth's "spontaneous overflow of powerful feelings" are misleading if we fail to notice Clare's quite different emphasis. He stresses the integrity of poetry which arises from an individual mind rather than a tradition of art, which encompasses not a craftsman creating novel "objets d'art," but real expressions of personal experience. When we remember that Clare regarded natural objects as the only suitable material for mental speculation, it becomes clear that what flows from the mind will be natural objects or scenes altered by the individual mind into appropriate metaphoric or symbolic form.

When discussing Clare's concept of the poem, we must bear in mind that he believed thoughts, not words, were the proper medium for expression. The image is not merely concrete, and therefore definable by a single word, but involves an abstract element which can only be conveyed through a combination of words which add up to a whole greater than the sum of its parts. For example, the effect of Clare's well-known portrait of the badger is not only contained in the special qualities of language he employs, or in associations inherent in the word "badger," but in the thoughts which arise from his cumulative description of the badger's appearance and actions. The dramatic situation and the action described in the following portion of that poem create a memorable picture of the embattled animal even though they are conveyed in simple, almost non-emotive diction and syntax:

> He falls as dead and kicked by boys and men
> Then starts and grins and drives the crowd agen
> Till kicked and torn and beaten out he lies
> And leaves his hold and cackles groans and dies.[70]

The syntax here, with its double repetition in the first line and triple repetition in the second, third, and fourth, reinforces the action and is more evocative than in most of the poem, but of all the words only "cackles" draws any attention to itself. The poem depends primarily on the image it presents to the mind, on our "seeing" and responding to an overall picture.

This is not to suggest that Clare ignored the right choice of word, or failed to realize the value of his craft as a writer, but only that he saw diction and syntax as subservient to the re-creation of a picture to which they contributed. His feelings were complex enough that he was constantly aware of the inadequacy of language to convey the full impact of his experience. A forlorn fragment recorded by W. F. Knight, the house steward at the Northampton Asylum while Claré was there, bears eloquent testimony to the failure of language to facilitate completely Clare's emotional message to the world:

> Language has not the power to speak what love indites
> The Soul lies buried in the Ink that writes.[71]

The real poem is what the poet uses words to convey, a mental phenomenon contained in thoughts and expressed only imper-

fectly through words. Even "paint itself with living nature fails
. . . and mind alone feels fancies and pourtrays."[72]

By thus directing the emphasis away from the verbal
composition of the poem to the thoughts that emerge from it,
Clare reaffirms his claim that grammatical rules are irrelevant to
poetry. He felt that "whatever is intelligible to others is grammar
& whatever is common sense is not far from carrectness,"[73] and
in a more colorful mood he vowed "grammar in learning is like
tyranny in government—confound the bitch I'll never be her
slave."[74] Since the formulation of proper syntactical structures
was not necessary to convey his pictures of nature, he felt
justified in condemning not only grammar, but poetic diction as
well. Although he championed the cause of rustic language,
notably in his debates with Charles Lamb, and was himself no
mean verbal craftsman, he was more concerned with shifting the
emphasis from the mode of expression to the object or scene or
event being described and to the thought which arose from the
contemplation of it.

Most of Clare's poems are only the end-product of the process
we have been looking at, the final static record of the metaphors
and symbols, as well as the resultant joy which the poetic process
creates, but within some of them we can see the emergence of
metaphors from Clare's contemplation of a scene. This is the case
in "The Flood," a poem typical of Clare's mature accomplishment. It appears on the surface to present a colorful but rather
inconsequential description of a flooding stream in three
fourteen-line stanzas. But examined more closely it reveals a
well-wrought work of art from which a statement of Clare's
insight into his personal predicament gradually unfolds.

The first seven lines of the poem establish not only the poet's
physical position and state of mind, but also our sense of some as-
yet-unexplained significance to both:

> On Lolham Brigs in wild and lonely mood
> Ive seen the winter floods their gambols play
> Through each old arch that trembled while I stood
> Bent oer its wall to watch the dashing spray
> As their old stations would be washed away
> Crash came the ice against the jambs and then
> A shudder jarred the arches.[75]

The resistant pose of the bridge radiates an aura of strength in which the poet himself exults:

> —yet once more
> It breasted raving waves and stood agen
> To wait the shock as stubborn as before.

The bridge affords protection for the poet from the ravaging stream, but at the same time allows him to feel its action—the bridge trembles, but remains unmoved. There follows a description of the stream's destructive power working on the surrounding land, of its attempted damage to the bridge, and of the controlling force of the bridge's "engulphing arches":

> —White foam brown crested with the russet soil
> As washed from new ploughd lands would dart beneath
> Then round and round a thousand eddies boil
> On tother side—then pause as if for breath
> One minute—and ingulphed—like life in death
>
> Whose wrecky stains dart on the floods away
> More swift then shadows in a stormy day
> Straws trail and turn and steady—all in vain
> The engulphing arches shoot them quickly through
> The feather dances flutters and again
> Darts through the deepest dangers still afloat
> Seeming as faireys whisked it from the view
> And danced it oer the waves as pleasures boat
> Light hearted as a merry thought in may.

From his vantage point on the bridge he then describes the appearance of the flood with its debris of bushes and rails, and in so doing begins to expose the metaphor which has been working, though submerged, since the beginning of the poem:

> Trays—uptorn bushes—fence demolished rails
> Loaded with weeds in sluggish motions stray
> Like water monsters lost each winds and trails
> Till near the arches—then as in affright
> It plunges—reels—and shudders out of sight.

This description of the monster's movements, deftly supported by a cacophonic sibilance, recalls the use of "gambols" in the opening lines and of subsequent words commonly associated with monsters. For example, the waves are "raving" one minute and pausing for breath the next, and are compared to "life in death" at one point. The action of the stream in uprooting trees and weeds is also suggestive of the activities of a monster. But at this stage of the poem the connection between the monster and the flood is extremely tenuous because it is only the debris that has been referred to as a monster. Clare makes the relationship complete in line twenty-nine, however, when he describes the waves' motion:

> Waves trough—rebound—and fury boil again
> Like plunging monsters rising underneath
> Who at the top curl up a shaggy main
> A moment catching at a surer breath
> Then plunging headlong down and down—and on
> Each following boil the shadow of the last
> And other monsters rise when those are gone
> Crest their fringed waves—plunge onward and are past.

It is important to notice here how the poet carefully invites us to observe that he has been using the submerged metaphor since early in the poem. He does this by repeating, in his description of the monster, images he has previously used to describe the waves. The crested wave of line thirty-six, for example, refers back to the "brown crested" foam of line ten, and "monsters pause for breath" in line thirty-two recalls the identical situation in line thirteen. The atmosphere has been created through an accumulation of such images which prepares the reader for the eventual disclosure of the metaphor.

At this point Clare returns to his own situation and its relationship to the metaphor:

> —The chill air comes around me ocean blea
> From bank to bank the waterstrife is spread
> Strange birds like snow spots oer the huzzing sea
> Hang where the wild duck hurried past and fled.

He depicts the desolation of his environment, here, in terms reminiscent of his opening description of a "wild and lonely mood," a portrayal which, by the ambivalence of its syntactical position, applies to both the poet and the flood. This dual

application is evident in the final couplet which discusses the
universal implications of the central metaphor:

> On roars the flood—all restless to be free
> Like trouble wandering to eternity.

Thus the initial experience has developed in the poet's mind to a
conclusion in which the entire experience becomes symbolic of a
larger truth. On the physical level he sees a turbulent flood,
filled with uprooted trees, battering the bridge upon which he
stands, and he feels the shock of this activity. On the level of
metaphor he sees a series of monsters confined by the arches of
the bridge—their very shape suggests a type of clamp which
holds them to the earth—restless and fighting to be free. And on
the universal level he pictures the restless, wandering, and
disruptive forces in the world struggling to an impasse with
stubborn, restricting, and stabilizing structures. The poet surveys
this "waterstrife" from the bridge which protects him from the
destructive forces, but allows him the sensitivity to feel their
vibrations without being destroyed. He identifies with the
restless element in mood and through his fascination with its
activity, but remains confident in his resistance to it.

Thus what appears to be a simple description is, in reality, a
complex and subtle exploration of two of the contraries of
existence, an exploration that employs description, metaphorization, and universalization. We can see the gradual emergence of
the metaphor as Clare contemplates and describes the scene. His
mind notices the similarity between what it sees and the image of
monsters with which it is already familiar. By fusing the two,
Clare not only creates a symbol out of the landscape, but also
injects into the landscape a life and meaning of its own. In a
sense, too, the stream looks up and gives him, not joy this time,
but a curious mixture of anxiety and confidence.

This poem is not an exceptional one in Clare's canon, nor does
it contain all his essential qualities, but it does serve as an
example of what he was doing with metaphor and language.

V   Rhyme and Polish

The impression left by Clare's comments on his method of
composition indicate he did not share Wordsworth's faith in the

efficacy of "emotion recollected in tranquility." The end of the process left Clare despondent, not tranquil, and he made every effort to record the experience as soon after it occurred as he could. As he told his publisher in a letter, "the Muse is a fickle Hussey with me she sometimes stilts me up to madness & then leaves me as a beggar by the wayside with no more life then whats mortal & that nearly extinguishd by mellancholy forbodings."[76] As a result, many of the poems which record the poetic process end in this kind of disappointment:

> Vain burns the soul and throbs the fluttering heart
> Their painfull pleasing feelings to impart
> Till by successles[s] sallies wearied quite
> The memory fails and fancy takes her flight
> The wickett nipt within its socket dies
> Born down and smother'd in a thousand sighs.[77]

The experience of composition is a transitory one which leaves behind a residue in the memory which itself gradually disappears. The extent to which Clare relied on the immediate experience and how bereft of his poetic powers its departure left him is illustrated by his comment in another letter to his publisher which included Clare's sonnet "To the Memory of John Keats":

I did it as I felt it at the moment your mellancholy news woud give me pause for reflection—I wishd I had made an Elegy afterwards of it as my ideas was crampt they flowd freely & I could have gone a great length but words are of little value—be as it will I can do nothing more now—the moment is gone I cannot call it back I wish I coud.[78]

As a result of experiences like this, the composition of Clare's poems took place as much as possible during or immediately after the rapturous experience itself. He is specific about his method in his autobiography. "Poetry," he writes, "was a troublesomely pleasant companion annoying & cheering me at my toils I coud not stop my thoughts & often faild to keep them till night so when I fancyd I had hit upon a good image or natural description I usd to steal into a corner of the garden & clap it down."[79] This was his procedure early in his career as he reminds Taylor in a letter: "reccolect the subjects are roughly sketchd in the fields at all seasons with a pencil I catch nature in every dress she puts on so when I begin to rhyme & polish up I have little to do in studying."[80] And he followed a similar routine to the end of his career. A fellow patient at the Northampton asylum observed that "one principle article [which Clare carried with him] was an octavo sheet or two of paper, whereon to write his thoughts, chiefly Poems, which he wrote in his leisure moments, for his mind seemed ever on the alert, when seated alone for any length of time."[81] Most of these sheets of paper have not survived as his earlier notes have, so we cannot be sure of the extent to which Clare revised in the asylum years, but we will see in a later chapter that as late as 1841 he thought it necessary to extensively rearrange *Child Harold*.

The immediacy of this method resulted in an acknowledged influence of the poet's environment and personal mood at the time of composition on the poem produced. We cannot, of course, be sure what his situation was while composing all of the poems, but most of them, like most Romantic poems, were descriptive of actual experiences. Consequently, these influences are often woven into the fabric of the poem. His nature poems are almost always situational and even many of the songs, excluding the traditional ballads which he refurbished, betray the situation of the poet at the time of composition. Even his narratives are frequently descriptive of personal experiences. Of "Michaelmas Eve," for example, Clare writes, "I was one of the assembly & these three figures gave me the hint for the poem & every incident in it is truth & drawn from the life."[82] So the immediate experience had a considerable influence on the final product, even to the extent of whether Clare expressed himself in poetry or prose: "my feelings were stirred into praise & my praises were mutterd in prose or rhyme as the mood might suit at the moment."[83] Often, as we shall see later, the meter of a piece was influenced by the "dancing measure" Clare had in his head at the time or the sound of his mother's spinning wheel near him as he wrote.[84] His dependence on an immediate transcription of the experience also meant that he could not successfully write to order. In a letter to Frank Simpson in 1828, he explains his failure to write an epitaph for one of Simpson's friends:

Its all no use I can do nothing for the more I try the worse I am & the reason why it is is I believe that I never knew Mr. Friar & therfore I cannot feel the subject at all so here I give it up with much reluctance.[85]

His failure to compose this epitaph stems from the absence of a severe enough personal feeling of grief, a feeling which *was* real to him on Keats's death even though he knew him only indirectly. The immediate mood was crucial in composing the sonnet on Keats's death.

What Clare jotted down immediately was seldom the final form his poem took, however. If there was no period of rumination between the experience and the composition as there was in Wordsworth's method, there was at least a period of extensive revision which often saw the poem change shape several times. Some poems, too, were composed from several jottings and memories which coalesced over a period of time into a unified composition. One such poem is "Pleasant Places," several drafts of which are scattered throughout Clare's notebooks. It appears first[86] on a loose sheet of paper as an untitled draft of twenty-four lines, the first ten of which describe a scene visually, with the remaining fourteen focusing on the simultaneously perceived song of blackbirds:

> This leaning tree with ivy over hung
> This crooked brook oer which is rudely flung
> A slender plank that bends beneath the feet
> And that small hill the shepherds summer seat
> Make up a picture to the mind and wear
> A nobler gild than pallace walls can heir
> To me the wild wind dashes oer the scene
> Enchantments shades of vivifying green
> I see her sketchy pencil in her hand
> Painting the moving scene to fairy land
> That blackbirds music from this hazel bower
> Turns into golden drops this summer shower
> To think the rain that moists his sutty wing
> Should wake the gushes of his soul to sing
> Hark at the melody how rich and loud
> Like daylight breaking thro the morning cloud
> How luscious thro that sea of green it floats
> Knowst that of music breaks from sweeter notes
> Than that wild minstrel of the summer shower
> Breaths at this moment from that hazel bower
> To me the anthem of a thousand tongues
> Were poor and idle to the simple songs
> Of that high toned and edifying bird
> That sings to nature music by itself unheard

That he is describing a specific scene is obvious from his use of the present tense and his insistent reference to specific objects, as well as from his stressing the unity of the visual and auditory aspects of the scene coming together "at this moment." But for all his attempts to unite the two sections of the poem, they remain distinct, the second heading off in a new direction marked not only by a different imagery, sound rather than sight imagery, but a quite different theme.

When Clare took the poem up again he condensed it into a unified sonnet by expunging all references to the blackbird's song and reworking the four lines about the wind to reemphasize and complete the visual quality of the opening lines.[87] Although he experiments with six lines about the blackbird in the left- and righthand margins of this manuscript, he does not insert them into the poem. Apart from replacing the first line with a line that appears as an isolated line in a different manuscript, eliminating the incongruous reference to palace walls, and tidying up some of the phraseology, he also changes from an individual experience to a general one. The specific pronouns "this" and "that" are replaced by a general, plural listing of objects: "cold stonepits," "crooked brooks," and "narrow lanes." And he stresses the universal appeal of these objects by inserting a new line which interrelates all of them: "These are the picturesque of taste to me." The original experience that produced the twenty-four-line draft recedes as Clare works his material into a general statement of his aesthetic preferences. Two other drafts,[88] one of them adding a title for the first time, improve some lines and replace a few words, but do not alter the basic character of the poem that appears, finally, as a polished and mature expression of Clare's pleasure in natural objects when under the influence of the blending motion of the wind:

> Old stonepits with veined ivy overhung
> Wild crooked brooks oer which is rudely flung
> A rail and plank that bends beneath the tread
> Old narrow lanes where trees meet over head
> Path stiles on which a steeple we espy
> Peeping and stretching in the distant sky
> And heaths oerspread with furze blooms sunny shine
> Where wonder pauses to exclaim 'divine'
> Old ponds dim shadowed with a broken tree

> These are the picturesque of taste to me
> While painting winds to make compleat the scene
> In rich confusion mingles every green
> Waving the sketchy pencil in their hands
> Shading the living scenes to fairy lands.[89]

What appears to have little basis in a specific poetic experience is actually the culmination of a long process of revision that began with Clare's personal response to an individual scene. The poetic process created the original fragment; Clare's craftsmanship molds that into a coherent poem.

While this method produced the bulk of Clare's poetry, it was not his sole resource. When these intense experiences came less frequently to him, as a result either of their chronological distance in the past or from his eventual physical removal from nature, he was forced to rely on memory or on vicarious experiences. He often expressed his gratitude for the power of memory, as he does in "The Tell-Tale Flowers": "And from the brook I turned away, / but heard it many an after day."[90] But he also accepts that it is only the shadow of the original experience: "The spring of our life—our youth—is the midsummer of our happiness—our pleasures are then real & heart stirring—they are but associations afterwards . . .—our minds only retain the resemblance."[91]

That Clare was conscious of using this method is revealed by his prose comments, in which he continually refers to having composed songs and poems from memory, as well as by several of his poems. In "Ashton Lawn" he describes how his pictorial method of perception in the initial experience serves as a means of preserving the sensation for future exploitation:

> I had a joy and keep it still alive
> Of hoarding in the memorys treasured book
> Old favourite spots that with affections thrive
> And to my inward fancys shine and look
> Like well-done pictures in some winning page.[92]

The memory retains the sensations in the form of a picture, or static moment captured from a succession of scenes or situations, and makes them available later for reproduction into poems. He does not describe in any detail the mental process that follows the rejuvenation of the picture, but this is presumably because it is the same process of excitement (though on a reduced scale) and of composition as that which follows the initial perception of other images.

Although he was at times capable of composing to order—his letters contain several pleas for subject matter to try his talents—by far the bulk of his poetry, and that the most accomplished of it, was composed during either a direct poetic experience or an indirect simulation of the original. The result of these methods of composition is poetry that is highly metaphoric, since derived from a process of perception which "saw" natural objects as metaphors or symbols, and highly personal, since based almost exclusively on individual experiences of the poet in nature.

CHAPTER 3

The Poetic Process as Structure

CLARE'S method of perception provided him with both content and form for much of his nature poetry. The content was drawn from his personal experiences wandering through the fens or working in the fields, and much of the form, like that of "The Flood" and the sonnets already mentioned, arose out of his special way of viewing natural objects. From the character of his poetic experiences he derived a form which eventually gave him the means of coherently structuring what naturally tended to be rambling, discursive, and loosely organized poems. And from his observation that the mind extracted metaphors out of contemplated nature he developed an increasingly mature handling of imagery and image patterns. The development is from generally discursive poems with conventional and isolated meaphors to more clearly structured works containing natural imagery often arranged into unifying patterns.

Clare's literary career can be divided into reasonably distinct periods to illustrate this growth. Since few of his poems can be dated with any degree of accuracy, however, establishing chronological relationships between individual poems within a period is virtually impossible. Consequently, these periods will be treated here as units to be compared and contrasted with each other, but not, unfortunately, to demonstrate development within themselves. As we shall see, Clare's literary life falls into four stages: two Helpston periods, the first from 1809 to 1824 and the second from 1824 to 1832; the Northborough period from 1832 to 1841, including his three years in the asylum at High Beech and his few months of freedom in 1841; and the years from 1842 to 1864 which he spent in the Northamptonshire asylum.

I   *1809 to 1824*

The first of these periods extends from his employment at Francis Gregory's Bluebell Inn, which he later called "the nursery for that lonely & solitary musing which ended in rhyme,"[1] to his first major symptoms of physical and mental illness, and his consequent consultation with Dr. Darling in London, fifteen years later. This visit to London provides a convenient dividing point because it was preceded by a period of complete mental exhaustion during which all composition was suspended. The period includes his publication in 1820 of *Poems Descriptive of Rural Life and Scenery* and in 1821 of *The Village Minstrel and Other Poems*, as well as three of his trips to London and his resulting acquaintance with such literary personalities as Lamb, Hazlitt, Coleridge, and De Quincey. It was characterized by fits of creativity, notably in the summer of 1820, the spring of 1822, and January to June of 1823, interspersed with bouts of extreme depression and almost total abstinence from the muse, especially in 1821 when Clare was anxious at the long delay in the publication of *The Village Minstrel*, and in 1824 when mental exhaustion brought him to despair. It embraced the heights of Clare's popularity after the appearance of his first volume, and the depths of his isolation and loneliness following the failure of his second. And it contained a wealth of experimentation with poetic subjects and forms, as evidenced in his attempts at satire, narratives, songs, sonnets, ballads, and nature poems.

This period was also marked by considerable experimentation with the use of an immediate experience as a structuring device for his poems. The title of his first poem, "Morning Walk," suggests that his method came naturally to him, probably arising from both his personal preference for rambling in the fields around Helpston and, as Mark Storey has demonstrated, from his early reading of similar poems by James Thomson and others.[2] At any rate his early poetry contains glimpses of what was later to develop into coherent and unified poems built on a framework of the poet's personal experiences. For the moment, however, his experimentation produced only a very clumsy and often embarrassingly naïve use of the experience. Seldom tracing the progress of his aesthetic response to nature, he was content to restrict himself to physical situations from which he viewed the landscape, or to rambling walks which would connect several scenes into the scope of a single experience. Any meditative passage in these poems is usually a short segment sharply distinct from the action described, though often related to something perceived during the walk.

Most of the weaknesses of his early work are evident in "Lines Written in a Summer Evening."[3] Although there is a suggestion of unity in the chronological sequence of the observer's description, the poem lacks the focus usually provided by the physical situation of the poet. It shifts from one scene to another with no sense of being viewed through the single window of his mind. We see characters and objects outdoors which are ostensibly related to his position by his distinguishing between "far and near," but we also see Dobson preparing for bed *inside* his cottage. Only in the final eight lines is the poet's location established:

> Now, as stretching o'er the bed,
> Soft I raise my drowsy head
> Listening to the ushering charms
> That shake the elm tree's mossy arms
> Till sweet slumbers stronger creep
> Deeper darkness stealing round
> Then as rock'd, I sink to sleep
> Mid the wild wind's lulling sound.

If the activity portrayed in the rest of the poem has been directly perceived by the poet, the concluding lines must involve a change of location—since he is now in bed—from one which has not even been established. Nor is his description of the external scene limited to a reasonable selection of what one person is likely to see from a given position; it is crammed full with at least twenty-three varieties of birds and animals as well as ten human beings, and it begs for selectivity or artistic economy. Ironically, when the poet does enter the poem his presence is an unwelcome intrusion. His indignant outburst against mischievous boys and his burdensome moralizing on Providence, although they do arise out of the events described, do not give the impression of being provoked by his immediate experience, as the sentiment in "The Flood" does. They appear instead as abruptly inserted, made-to-order platitudes. This inability to fuse the objectivity of the observer and the subjectivity of the commentator is particularly evident in these early poems and is overcome in the later works by stressing the subjectivity resulting from the limited perceptions of a single observer.

In another early poem Clare attempts to link the multiplicity of scenes he wants to describe by more clearly relating them to his own activity. "Recollections after a Ramble"[4] is a series of very loosely connected descriptive passages, rich in variety, but linked by being perceived through the constantly moving focus of the poet's eye. Clare alleviates the impression of a cluttered landscape by admitting that the scenes are not viewed from a fixed point and that the movement from scene to scene is a progressive one, based, however loosely, on his own physical movements. Depiction of his personal role remains awkward, however, and is interspersed, rather than integrated with the rest of the poem. For the most part he describes his actions and his perceptions alternately, in no way fusing the significance of both, although at some points in the poem he does relate them by noticing a causal relationship between them:

> And as while I clum the hill
> Many a distant charm I found
> Pausing on the lagging mill
> That scarcly movd its sails around
> Hanging oer a gate or stile
> Till my curious eye did tire
> Leisure was employd awhile
> Counting many a peeping spire.

Near the end of the poem he demonstrates his awareness that his rambling has given the poem a semblance of order by bringing to his attention the scenes that comprise the poem:

> Be the journey ere so mean
> Passing by a cot or tree
> In the rout there's somthing seen
> Which the curious love to see
> In each ramble tastes warm souls
> More of wisdoms self can view
> Than blind ignorance beholds
> All lifes seven stages through.

The fact remains, however, that the poem lacks a real sense of unity, and the rambling nature of the experience itself is insufficient to provide coherence to the material it gathers.

"Recollections after an Evening Walk,"[5] although less satisfactory from a metrical standpoint, adheres more closely to the restrictions imposed by the poet's limited perspective and consequently eliminates not only the overcrowded scenery, but also the inconsistency which results from an omniscient author in a limited physical location. Thus elements of the scene move out of his range of perception, both visually and audibly:

> The mower too lapt up his scyth from our sight
> And put on his jacket and bid us good night
> The thresher once lumping we heard him no more
> He left his barn dust and shut up his door.

And others are brought to his attention not by the whim of an all-seeing mind, but by their emergence upon his immediately visible landscape:

> And numbers of creatures apeard in our sight
> That live in the silence and sweetness of night
> Climbing up the tall grasses or scaling the bough
> But these were all namless unnoticd till now.

Clare is more conscious in this poem, too, of the necessity of making his own actions more consonant with his descriptions, hence clearer to his reader. He opens the poem, therefore, with an outline of its ensuing structure:

> Just as the even bell rung we set out
> To wander the fields and the meadows about
> And the first thing we markt that was lovly to view
> Was the sun hung on nothing and bidding adieu.

He not only establishes the central situation, in these lines, but also suggests that the movement of the poem will be a wandering one involving a series of perceptions subsequent to his initial remarking of the sun. He enforces his own presence in the poem with allusions to the anticipated effect of his footsteps on a worm, and with direct reminders of his movements: "then we

wound round 'neath the brooks willow row" and "then we turn'd
up by the rut rifted lane." Appropriately, the poem is forced to a
conclusion by the conditions he established in the opening lines.
An evening walk is, by definition, limited and Clare accepts this
limitation for his poem as well:

> And then we turnd up by the rut rifted lane
> And sought for our cot and the village again
> For night gatherd round and shut all from the eye
> And a black sutty cloud crept all over the sky.

When the poet can no longer see, he ceases to write; his poem is
governed by the perceptions that his walk will allow him.

Although the experience in this poem is often overwhelmed by
description of country scenes, it does tend to aid Clare in
selecting his material and organizing it in the work itself.
Significantly, though, this experience is not a mental one. He
describes no process of selection, rapture, and metaphorization,
nor does he reveal the precise incident that caused him to write
the poem. Thus the form seems not to have grown directly out of
the event. Mastery of this technique was to come later, although
a few poems of this period attempt to use description of a poetic
experience as a framework for composition.

Such a poem is "Narrative Verses."[6] Although the poet's
response to nature is not always obvious in it, we can detect an
effort to convey the mental experience he is going through, and
to describe the poetic process as it transforms the landscape
through which he walks. After the second stanza establishes the
situation of solitude, the third records the selective activity of
taste reacting to nature's beauties:

> The glowing landscapes charms, I caught
>   Where ere I look't, or wander'd oer,
> And every wood, and field, me thought
>   A greener, brighter, prospect wore.

A description of the ideal state of mind for a poetic transformation of the scene follows. What he requires is,

> A vacant, opening in my mind;
>   To think, and cherish, thy fond scenes . . .

> Sometimes, musing on the skie,
> Then list'ning to the waterfall.

And eventually his rumination climaxes in the inevitable mental excitement:

> But O! so tempting was the muse
> She made me wish; she made me hope
> I wish'd and hop'd that future days
> (For scenes prophetic fill'd my breast)
> Whould grant to me a Crown of bays
> By singing maids and shepherds drest.

In spite of the apparent continuity of the process when examined in isolation, it fails to give a similar coherence to the poem. Clare does not yet allow the experience to govern the composition; consequently he includes several descriptions that are not related to the mental response itself. He also includes irrelevant details which contradict the generally pleasant mood of his reflections on nature, details such as this expression of fear:

> [I] watch the owners, of the grounds,
> Their presence, was my only fear;
> No boughs, to shield me, if they came,
> And soon, amid my rash career,
> I deem'd such trespasing, to blame.

His digression (it continues for another stanza) bears no relation to the poetic activity he is describing and, although it actually formed part of his observations while walking to Burghley Park on the day he wrote the poem, it is irrelevant to the main progression of his mind from initial perception, to rapture, to the desire for composition. For all its weaknesses, though, this is perhaps the most successful poem of its type in Clare's early work.

Clare's images in this period are often stereotyped, rising out of literary convention rather than his individual response to nature. Unlike "The Flood," where the metaphor of a monster emerges from an accumulation of terms used to describe the stream, thus giving a coherent picture of physical and metaphysical destruction, his early poems abound in metaphors imposed upon them from without. In "Summer Evening" there is a conglomeration of individual metaphors which, when they are not simply idiomatic expressions, are used to illuminate isolated objects with no relation either to each other or to an overall plan. The poem includes the conventional personifications of Providence, ignorance, and sleep, but, with the exception of a fascinating picture of a bat "in hood and cowl," there is very little metaphor beyond the "murmuring" brook and "sleeping" flowers. A similar lack of pattern characterizes "Recollections after an Evening Walk" in which the individual metaphors are more colorful, but fail to convince us that the poetic process creates rather than imposes metaphors. "To an Insignificant Flower"[7] attempts to form a pattern of metaphor by equating the flower with Emma, beauty, a swain, and the poet, but the result is a naïve and obviously contrived lyric. More evidence of experimenting with image patterns can be found in "Recollections after a Ramble," where a series of references to the lark's "anthem," the wood's "song," birds' "songs," and nature's "anthem" suggests an underlying metaphoric structure. The references are too few for a poem of this length, however, and not clearly enough related to each other or to a central metaphor to be considered an effective pattern.

The first Helpston period, then, is notable for experimentation and limited achievement in the use of a personal experience to give form and substance to Clare's poetry. The reputation he established in his first two volumes of verse was founded more on minute observation of his natural environment and intimate knowledge of rustic life than on the technical competence of a poet mature in his craft. He had, by this time, formulated much of his evolving theory of poetry, however, and the years that followed saw him create his own style from his personal response to nature.

II   *1824 to 1832*

Following his return from London in 1824, Clare embarked on a period of prolific composition in both prose and verse. He began an autobiography, a journal, numerous essays and poems, and a series of "Natural History Letters" which he planned to publish under the title *Biographies of Birds and Flowers.* His industry was interrupted by anxiety at the delays in publication of *The Shepherd's Calendar,* however, and several of these projects remain incomplete. In November of 1825 he published his essay on "Popularity in Authorship" in *The European Magazine,* and in the period 1824–27 he published several poems in imitation of older poets. But his remaining years at Helpston were filled with unsuccessful attempts at prose works such as a tragedy in the style of Christopher Marlowe on "Jealousy" or "Conscience," of which he wrote only four hundred lines, a novel which exists only in fragments, and two incomplete prose tales, "The Stage Coach" and "The Two Soldiers." He began a collection of old ballads and folksongs about this time, too, and wrote well over a hundred sonnets, a large number of which are occasional pieces but several of which, including "The Flood" and "Snow Storm," are among his best works. The period also includes his fourth visit to London in February–March of 1828. He returned from this visit compelled to peddle his own books around the countryside to support his family, and advised by Alan Cunningham that for health reasons, he should cease his writing. He followed that advice for most of 1828 and 1829. In the following year his increasing physical and mental illness resulted in a public outburst against Shylock at a Peterborough performance of *The Merchant of Venice* and his plight consequently gained the attention of the local gentry. The eventual result was their provision of the new cottage at Northborough and Clare's removal to it in May, 1832.

The poetry he composed at Helpston between 1824 and 1832 reveals a more sophisticated use of the experience as a structural device and a more confident utilization of metaphor. Although many poems of this period have a tendency to ramble without a controlling structure, others indicate an increasing adherence on Clare's part to the truth of the experience, a tendency to dwell on mental activities rather than on physical ones, and a conscious attempt to demonstrate within the poem how it arose from the poet's actual perception. And although he often uses conventional metaphors expressed through archaic diction and syntax, he increasingly derives his imagery from the scene he is describing. This results not only in a much more natural mode of description, uniquely his own, but also in a unity and economy superior to the earlier works.

We can see his growing skill at subordinating pure description to personal response by comparing "Autumn" and "Walks in the

Woods." The former,[8] in spite of its departure from the
simplicity of Clare's usual diction, is one of the finest pieces of
the period. It is elicited from a personal experience which is
conveyed economically by linking the descriptive passages
without detailing the poet's superfluous movements, as Clare so
often did in his earlier work. The poet enters the poem by
moving into "solitudes . . . to meditate [autumn's] end." As he
executes this movement he describes the setting, linking the
several elements of the scene syntactically, by combining the
four stanzas that describe them into a single deftly wrought
sentence:

> Syren of sullen moods and fading hues
> Yet haply not incapable of joy
> > Sweet autumn I thee hail
> > With welcome all unfeigned
> And oft as morning from her lattice peeps
> To beckon up the sun I seek with thee
> > To drink the dewy breath
> > Of fields left fragrant then
>
> To solitudes where no frequented paths
> But what thine own feet makes betray thy home
> > Stealing obtrusive there
> > To meditate thine end
> By overshadowed ponds in woody nooks
> With ramping sallows lined and crowding sedge
> > Who woo the winds to play
> > And with them dance for joy
>
> And meadow pools torn wide by lawless floods
> Where water lilies spread their oily leaves
> > On which as wont the flye
> > Oft battens in the sun
> Where leans the mossy willow half way oer
> On which the shepherd crawls astride to throw
> > His angle clear of weeds
> > That crowd the waters brim
>
> Or crispy hills and hollows scant of sward
> Where step by step the patient lonely boy
> > Hath cut rude flights of stairs
> > To climb their steepy sides

> Then tracking at their feet grown hoarse with noise
> The crawling brook that ekes its weary speed
> And struggles thro the weeds
> With faint and sullen brawls.

This sentence demonstrates the functional role of Clare's description because it is composed of a series of clauses, each beginning with a conjunction and describing a specific component of the scene, subordinated to the main, active clauses "I seek with thee" and "stealing obtrusive there." It contains no random sights that just happen to have formed part of Clare's walk, but ingredients that are necessary to convey the precise mood of his relationship with the goddess autumn. Clare explains the impulse that has caused him to extract his poem from his immediate experience in the next stanza:

> These haunts long favoured but the more as now
> With thee thus wandering moralizing on
> Stealing glad thoughts from grief
> And haply tho I sigh
> Sweet vision with the wild dishevelled hair
> And raiments shadowy of each winds embrace
> Fain would I win thine harp
> To one accordant theme.

Clare's mental response at a particular time, "now," is the direct source of the poem, since the direct result of his desire to emulate the wind's music. And the experience takes place primarily in the mind:

> We'll pillow on the grass
> Our thoughts and ruminate
> Oer the disordered scenes of woods and fields.

Clare continues from here with a series of scenes that are rooted in the immediate experience, since they provide material for his rumination, and he concludes with a direct address to the personified autumn:

> Wild sorceress me thy restless mood delights
> More than the stir of summers crowded scenes

> Where jostled in the din
> Joy pauled mine ear with song
> Heart sickening for the silence that is thine
> Not broken inharmoniously as now
> That lone and vagrant bee
> Booms faint its weary chime
>
> And filtering winds thin winnowing thro the woods
> In tremelous noise that bids at every breath
> Some sickly cankered leaf
> Let go its hold and die
> And now the bickering storm with sudden start
> In flirting fits of anger carpeth loud
> Thee urging to thine end
> Sore wept by troubled skyes.

The address continues for another three stanzas before it concludes in Clare's anticipation of the death of his goddess.

Since the central experience of "Autumn" is a poetic one, we can trace the movement from casual observation to rapture, to metaphorization, and finally to the desire for composition. Although not presented in that order, these steps are identified in the poem, thereby forming a bond between the experience and the poem it produces. The culmination of this process, the transformation of the scene, is summed up in the following stanza:

> And yet sublime in grief thy thoughts delight
> To show me visions of most gorgeous dyes
> Haply forgetting now
> They but prepare thy shroud
> Thy pencil dashing its excess of shades
> Improvident of waste till every bough
> Burns with thy mellow touch
> Disorderly divine.

The metaphor extracted from the season is reimposed on it and fused with it to enhance Clare's response. The instantaneous combination in his mind of autumn as a goddess and of the actual scene he perceives transforms the landscape into an appropriately "divine" state. The extent of this fusion can be measured by examining its influence on the ostensibly "pure" description of scenery. The major characteristic of the goddess, her "wild *dishevelled* hair" (my italics), is reflected in the details of even the most prosaic activities of nature and man: in the "disordered scenes of woods and fields," the "rambling bramble berries," the "half indolent" cowherd, and the "vagrant bee."

The language itself reflects this fusion, combining without the slightest hint of incongruity the elegant rhetoric of archaic diction with the simplicity of descriptive phrases like "where water lilies spread their oily leaves," and the evocative poetry of "filtering winds thin winnowing thro the woods" with the entirely assimilated dialect words such as "ramping" and "curdled." All elements of the poem coalesce into an evocative picture of autumn, and subside into a marvelous evocation of waning life. The wind "in tremelous noise . . . bids at every breath / Some sickly cankered leaf / Let go its hold and die." Physical death merges with the melancholy, but paradoxically sanguine, departure of the season:

> Thy life is waining now and silence tries
> To mourn but meets no sympathy in sounds
>   As stooping low she bends
>   Forming with leaves thy grave
> To sleep inglorious there mid tangled woods
> Till parch lipped summer pines in drought away
>   Then from thine ivied trance
>   Awake to glories new.

Although Clare demonstrates here and in several other poems of this period his ability to exploit the immediate experience for an artistic purpose, he does not do so consistently. For example, "Walks in the Woods,"[9] though an obvious improvement over poems of the first Helpston period, displays only a casual connection between descriptive passages. On the other hand, we are now constantly reminded that the poem's scope is limited by the poet's physical range of perception, even though he breaks out of this limitation into digressions which undermine the structure. In addition, the experience described is a mental one, although there is only passing reference to, and partial development of, the poetic process. The following lines, for instance, suggest the mental nature of his activities, but are not extended to the rest of the poem:

> — O I love
> To sit me there till fancy weaves
> Rich joys beneath a world of leaves
>
> Its moss stump grows the easiest chair
> Agen its grains my back reclines
> And woodbines twisted fragrance there
> In many a yellow cluster shines
> The lonesome bees that hither stray
> Seem travellers that loose their way.

Out of his rumination the moss stump becomes a metaphorical chair and the bees become travellers, but unlike the images in "Autumn" they merge in no controlling metaphor. Nor does this poem develop directly out of the poetic experience; there is no suggestion of the impulse to composition which produced the poem. On the contrary, Clare implies a denial of the possibility of expression, rejecting the possibility of a connection between the experience and the artistic expression of it:

> A rapture rushes at the heart
> A joy comes flushing in the face
> I feel so glad I cant explain
> My joy and on I rush again.

Having reached this point in the mental experience, Clare relapses to the physical as he rushes on through the woods. The poem is finally brought to an end by the conclusion of the experiences, but within the poem there is no developed tie between them and the poem itself.

The token gesture toward deriving metaphors out of the situation in "Walks in the Woods" is characteristic of Clare's experimentation in this period and is repeated continually in the poetry of these years. The following example from "Pastoral Fancies"[10] by its very awkwardness illustrates both his desire to extract imagery from the immediate scene and his limited progress to date:

> My rod and line doth all neglected lye
> A higher joy mine former sport destroys
> Nature this day doth bait the hook and I
> The glad fish am thats to be caught there bye.

We can be forgiven if we are reminded, here, of metaphysical poetry. The conceit is artificial in its expression, but it does obviously spring to his mind from his personal situation at the time. Clare's attempt to be "literary" betrays his lack of confidence in his own ability to elicit images from nature.

The most successful poems of the period, however, overcome his diffidence. "Snow Storm"[11] is the product of a confident poet who hints at a comprehensive symbol without the need to labor his point. Tibble publishes this poem as two sonnets, but it is obvious from the second sonnet's reliance on the first for its intelligibility that Clare intended the two to constitute one twenty-eight-line, two-stanza poem. Considered as such, it reveals a physical experience which merges into a imaginative one and in the process develops a metaphor out of the physical appearance of the scene. In the first half of the poem we see the active agency of winter "spreading" its influence over the landscape. The snow corresponds to the imagination, both the poet's "pliant eye" and the ordinary man's "dullest eyes," which "shapes" the real world into an imaginary one:

> Winter is come in earnest and the snow
> In dazzling splendour—crumping underfoot
> Spreads a white world all calm and where we go
> By hedge or wood trees shine from top to root
> In feathered foliage flashing light and shade
> Of strangest contrast—fancys pliant eye
> Delighted sees a vast romance displayed
> And fairy halls descended from the sky
> The smallest twig its snowy burthen wears
> And woods oer head the dullest eyes engage
> To shape strange things where arch and pillar bears
> A roof of grains fantastic arched and high
> And little shed beside the spinney wears
> The grotesque zemblance of an hermitage.

We move from the reality of "crumping" snow to the metaphor of a small shed transformed into a romantic hermitage. The action of nature, in the form of snow, parallels the transforming propensity of the mind, the whole stanza providing an explanation of how the concept of a hermitage grew out of Clare's observation of a winter scene. In the second half of the poem, the

imagination enlarges the metaphor until it completely dominates
and enriches our response to the scene:

On[e] almost sees the hermit from the wood
Come bending with his sticks beneath his arm
And then the smoke curl up its dusky flood
From the white little roof his peace to warm
One shapes his books his quiet and his joys
And in romances world forgetting mood
The scene so strange so fancys mind employs
It seems heart aching for his solitude
Domestic spots near home and trod so oft
Seen daily—known for years—by the strange wand
Of winters humour changed—the little croft
Left green at night when morns loth look obtrudes
Trees bushes grass to one wild garb subdued
Are gone and left us in another land.

The hermit is now the point of departure for Clare's imagination,
not simply the product of it. Significantly he is only "almost"
seen, and the details of his life are "shaped" by the mind. Such
qualification eliminates the charge of being untrue to the
experience, of describing things not actually perceived, which
was so easily levelled against his less mature work. By the end of
the poem the snow has silently assumed a symbolic role, fusing
natural forces with imaginative ones, so that the transformation
described in the final lines is an ambivalent one. It reflects the
power of nature and of the imagination. Clare's confidence in the
fusion is reinforced by the fact that he returns in these lines to
the vocabulary of physical description, relying on his already
established bond between snow and the mind to make his point
about transformation clear. The imagination, like snow,
transforms ordinary objects into metaphor and this metaphor is
derived not from the storehouse of conventional images which
supplied Clare previously—and often in this period, too—but
from the real experience upon which the poem is based.

Development, then, is the key word in a discussion of the
second Helpston period, development revealed in a few
consummately handled works rather than in a large number of
mature poems. Clare by 1832 was relying more on mental
experiences than physical, more on natural images than on

artificially contrived metaphors, and more on relating the poem and the image to the impulse from which they arose.

III   The Shepherd's Calendar

Clare's major achievement during this period was *The Shepherd's Calendar*,[12] a poem which many critics have hailed as his masterpiece. Eric Robinson and Geoffrey Summerfield call it "the truest poem of English country life ever written,"[13] and John Barrell compares it favorably with the sonnets, approving it as Clare's best expression of his pervasive and remarkably accurate "sense of place."[14] Mark Storey bases his enthusiasm for the poem on "the vigour of [Clare's] descriptions, his re-creation of a way of life, neither idealised nor sensationally realistic, but essentially loving."[15] These assessements reveal a good deal about Clare's descriptive style and his intense love for rural life, but they share the weakness of other critical opinions which view the poem as a sociological or anthropological document; they fail in the end to convince us that *The Shepherd's Calendar* is an effective poem.

Neither Barrell nor Robinson and Summerfield are primarily concerned with the formal structure of the poem, but Storey attempts to justify his appreciation of the poem by analyzing its form. Something of the difficulty of such an approach is evident in Storey's statement that "rather than impose a pattern on [his subject, Clare] lets one emerge."[16] In fact, the structure—the calendar—was imposed on it from the start, and the pattern that Storey claims to find never surfaces from the welter of detail and individual images he examines. Storey's explanation fails because we are never aware of a development in the poem beyond the obvious progress of the seasons and never convinced that the richness of Clare's observations and the abundance of teeming life he describes are controlled by a mature literary craftsman. *The Shepherd's Calendar* shows Clare groping for a form that will sustain a long descriptive poem and producing several interesting advances over the other, shorter, poems of this period, but never unifying his vision into an organic whole.

The calendar scheme itself offers a logical means of interrelating Clare's multifarious observations, but it soon grows tedious when not supported by other, less mechanical, devices. Clare

partially complements this method with recurring allusions to
various rural occupations as they alter throughout the year.
Ploughman, thresher, and hedger all appear in their appropriate
season and are linked by the shepherd who is active in one form
or another throughout the year. He fills center stage in June, his
busiest month, requiring the shearing of his flock and providing
him with the social pleasures of those who gather for that
activity. In July he is simply accessory to the scene, his own
activity dependent on completion of the haying which com-
mands most of the attention in that month. Even during the
harvest the shepherd is briefly remembered: "For shepherds are
no more of ease possest / But share the harvests labours with the
rest." This continuity of interest in the shepherd links each
month with the others and maintains a sense of progression.
Scrupulously adhered to, it could have provided the structure
the poem needs, but the richness and variety of life Clare wanted
to describe would hardly submit to such a restricting format.
What was required was a dominant form which would develop
out of the unique characteristics of each month, and a variety of
individual sections which would prevent monotony.

Within several of the months we can see Clare struggling to
find that form. The most obvious pattern he attempts to re-
create is the movement from dawn to dusk of a day typical to the
month. This attempt is apparent in "January," where he subtitles
the first section "A Winter's Day," and also in several other
months. January opens with the dispersal of winter laborers,
threshers, foddering boys, and shepherds to their work, while
the farmer muses "behind the tavern screen." We are given a
commentary on their simultaneous activities as they work
throughout the morning before we are introduced to schoolboys
making snowmen in their noon recess. This section concludes
with the evening return of workers in a passage effective for the
sense of convergence it transmits, as everyone is drawn toward
their evening fire:

> While maidens fresh as summer roses
> Joining from the distant closes
> Haste home wi yokes and swinging pail
> And thresher too sets by his flail
> And leaves the mice to peace agen . . .

The shepherd seeks his cottage warm
And tucks his hook beneath his arm
And weary in the cold to roam
Scenting the track that leadeth home
His dog wi swifter pace proceeds
And barks to urge his masters speed . . .
The hedger now in leathern coat
From woodland wilds and fields remote
After a journey far and slow
Knocks from his shoes the caking snow.

The section ends with a reminder that we have witnessed a typical January day in the life of rural laborers:

Thus doth the winters dreary day
From morn to evening wear away.

Most of the details in "January" are subordinated to this dominant movement and the final effect is one of symmetrical development and conclusion. In other months, however, this scheme is less satisfactorily employed. In "July," for example, we move through a long general segment on typical summer activities before this reference to morning promises a chronological organization to the section:

The pindar on the sabbath day
Soon as the darkness waxes grey
Before one sunbeam oer the ground
Spindles its light and shadow round
Goes round the fields at early morn.

We soon thereafter reach midday:

Noon gathers wi its blistering breath
Around and day dyes still as death
The breeze is stopt the lazy bough
Hath not a leaf that dances now.

There follows a lengthy description of evening pursuits, but the final effect is not one of symmetry so much as of a rather awkward, even casually introduced, adaptation of the daylight cycle to provide continuity to descriptions that are not organically held together.

Clare's most frequent method of description is a catalogue of effects which accumulate to impress a particular mood or sight on the reader. Although this method tends to give a miscellaneous quality to most sections of the poem, he utilizes it occasionally to organize the material in an entire "month." Such is the case in "May" where he justifies a series of catalogues by relating them to his personal practice of observing flowers in the field:

> My wild field catalogue of flowers
> Grows in my rhymes as thick as showers
> Tedious and long as they may be
> To some, they never weary me
> The wood and mead and field of grain
> I coud hunt oer and oer again
> And talk to every blossom wild
> Fond as a parent to a child
> And cull them in my childish joy
> By swarms and swarms and never cloy.

The remainder of this section is divided into catalogues of more flowers, of human activities, and of features of the landscape which bring pleasures in a Sunday walk. Clare's token explanation of his technique gives "May" a semblance of coherence that other months, plagued by list after list of flowers, scenes, and occupations, lack. Colorful as they are, these catalogues fail to give form to Clare's descriptions.

A more promising technique is suggested in the opening lines of "April," "May," and "July." All begin with the establishment of a controlling image: "July" is likened to a "daughter of pastoral smells and sights"; "May" to a "queen of months"; and "April" to a child:

> The infant april joins the spring
> And views its watery skye
> As youngling linnet trys its wing
> And fears at first to flye
> With timid step she ventures on
> And hardly dares to smile
> The blossoms open one by one
> And sunny hours beguile.

The metaphor here is enhanced by the ambiguity of the pronoun in the fifth line. The infant month is juxtaposed with the young linnet to suggest something of the timorous emergence of spring. In the two stanzas that follow, April is described in terms that are more obviously applicable to the month, but also suggest the gathering confidence of a young bird:

> And as the birds with louder song
> Each mornings glory cheers
> With bolder step she speeds along
> And looses all her fears
>
> In wanton gambols like a child
> She tends her early toils
> And seeks the buds along the wild
> That blossom while she smiles.

This imagery trails on into subsequent stanzas where Clare places his own "infant hours" into the context of the infant month, and where he refers to April as the "fairest child of spring." He concludes with an invocation to April to be his "yearly mate," and mourns her passing:

> And now thy sun is on the set
> Like to a lovely eve
> I view thy parting with regret
> And linger loath to leave.

The section has been divided into a third-person description of April and a direct address to her personified self, but both have been subordinated to the image of an infant. Unfortunately, the opening image in "July" is quickly forgotten and never returned to, and the personified queen and her court in "May" last only long enough to justify the initial catalogue of sounds in that month.

Other months, notably the three harvest months, reveal a more organically derived, less obviously imposed, structure. "August" has a single focus provided by the requirements of harvest which compel the whole community into a unified struggle to reap the grain. Thus Clare's description contains a corresponding focus which is counterbalanced by his division of the section into a typical work day and a typical sabbath day in

August. "September" is united by a pervading imagery of imprisonment and release which touches upon almost every activity in the section and relates them to the demanding labor of the fields. The blackbirds are "caged from out the sun," the children are "imprison'd" and mourn "for liberty and play." Even hogs "trye thro gates the street to gain," and ducks attempt to escape "nights dull prison." Numerous similar references are reinforced by suggestions of threatened violence which, while they do not actually imprison, at least provoke a desire for release and safety: the bees "threaten war to all that come," and in turn the old dame sets traps for the thieving hornet. Even the butterflies' present pleasure and the sparrow's song are measured by their contrast with previous danger: the former "flirts *unchaced* from flower to flower," and the latter sits "*unpelted* in the quiet street" (italics mine). The effect of these images in the early part of this section is to reinforce the motif of imprisonment, either present or past, in preparation for the release when work in the fields is completed. All, like the driving boy, are confined by time:

> While driving boy with eager eye
> Watches the church clock passing bye
> Whose gilt hands glitter in the sun
> To see how far the hours have run.

Evening, therefore, brings the desired escape; the second half of the section abounds in images of release. Children, now free from school, run to the fields to welcome their parents back from the completion of the harvest, the workers meet for their harvest supper, and those who have left their own occupation to assist in the fields are "reprieved" of their labor for another year.

"October" stands out from the other months in the calendar because its structure is derived from the "nature-walks" activity we have seen in other poems of the period. The structure develops out of Clare's method of perception, beginning with an explanation in the opening lines:

> Nature now spreads around in dreary hue
> A pall to cover all that summer knew
> Yet in the poets solitary way
> Some pleasing objects for his praise delay

> Somthing that makes him pause and turn again
> As every trifle will his eye detain.

This type of observation has been implied in other "months," but never overtly stated as his principle of organization. The details here have been selected by the poet's mind responding to natural images. It follows naturally, then, that he includes a catalogue of the scenes that arrest his attention. At one point in the catalogue he breaks off to remind us of his method:

> Such are the pictures that october yields
> To please the poet as he walks the fields.

At this point the succession of autumn scenes begins to coalesce into a metaphoric vision of nature, revealed in the image of a dying, but still beautiful, woman:

> While nature like fair woman in decay
> Which pale consumption hourly wastes away
> Upon her waining features pale and chill
> Wears dreams of beauty that seem lovely still.

From a profusion of individual objects the poet creates an encompassing metaphor which, when reapplied to the details of the scene, enhances their appeal and unites them in a complex vision of the beauty in autumnal nature. To accent this image Clare proceeds with another catalogue of delights, flirting with relevant images of "teazing" youths, fading trees, and moody winds. He concludes by summarizing the method he has used:

> These pictures linger thro the shortning day
> And cheer the lone bards mellancholy way
> And now and then a solitary boy
> Journeying and muttering oer his dreams of joy.

The structure of the "month" arises from his method of perception, culminating in the metaphor that his mind perceives in the accumulation of details.

Although this method of perception does not solve his structural problems outside "October," it clearly contributes to the special quality of his vision throughout *The Shepherd's*

Calendar. Details in individual passages are often united by being perceived through the wandering eye of the poet even though he does not always draw our attention to his presence in the scene. In the opening passage from "January," for example, he glances from the farmer in the tavern to the laborer "Pursu[ing] his way" to work, to the thresher and to the foddering boy. Each is described in sequence, though their actions are simultaneous, but each appears to be perceived from a single location. Likewise the return of figures from the distance at the end of the day suggests the observer is in the foreground where he has remained all day.

But a more profound quality of Clare's vision can be illustrated by these opening lines of "January." What distinguishes Clare's description in *The Shepherd's Calendar* from other descriptive verse is the constant tension he creates between an immediate personal view of a scene and the general or typical qualities he weaves into his tapestry of country life. The typical description always borders on the individual, frequently seducing us into the feeling that we are perceiving a specific scene. Something of this tension is apparent in the picture of a foddering boy early in "January":

> And foddering boys sojourn again
> By rhyme hung hedge and frozen plain
> Shuffling thro the sinking snows
> Blowing his fingers as he goes
> To where the stock in bellowings hoarse
> Call for their meals in dreary close
> And print full many a hungry track
> Round circling hedge that guards the stack
> Wi higgling tug he cuts the hay
> And bares the forkfull loads away
> And morn and evening daily throws
> The little heaps upon the snows.

The plural noun in the first line suggests a casual reference to any of a number of boys, but is soon narrowed to an individual boy three lines later. The singular is no grammatical slip; the details of the ensuing description are specific, concentrating on characteristic actions like "blowing his fingers" and cutting the hay with "higgling tug." Although the poet is portraying an individual, his picture becomes increasingly representative; the boy's actions occur at "morn and evening" rather than at the moment of perception. We end up with a single scene typical of others, but not, as we began with, a general description of foddering boys in a multitude of situations or locations. Shifts in number are common in Clare's rudimentary grammar, and they are often simply ambiguous, but many of them, especially when they move from plural to a repeated singular, indicate a corresponding shift in perspective. Thus lines like these contain a mere disregard for grammar:

> Whose glossy berrys picturesquly weaves
> Their swarthy bunches mid the yellow leaves.

But the description of foddering boys quite obviously, but subtly, shifts from the general to the individual to the representative.

This tension between the immediate and the general is reflected in Clare's propensity to describe general scenes in the progressive tense, giving them the appearance of happening while the poet records them, rather than at any time during the month and in any location. The boys, for example, "sojourn" in the first line, but Clare moves to the present participle when he shifts to the singular noun; the single boy is "snuffling" and "blowing." This same particularity is reflected in other descriptions by the adverb "now" as in "now fills the troughs for noisy hogs." The cumulative effect of this technique is a sense that we are witnessing the sports and occupations of Clare's rural characters while they are acted out, not as they are remembered by a chronicler of rural life. We also tend to see Clare's descriptions of natural objects not so much as general catalogues but as personal perceptions which we share. Both effects are the end product of Clare's poetic eye communicating as directly as he can what he actually sees.

Clare's method produces a wealth of individually striking images, images which capture the essence of the time of year he is describing: the bench in "September," for example, when the town has been deserted for the fields,

> The bench beneath its eldern bough
> Lined oer with grass is empty now.

or the plough which evokes the present idleness in "January" but also reminds us of the toil to come,

> While in the fields the lonly plough
> Enjoys its frozen sabbath now,

or the fog in "November" which subordinates all other elements of the scene to its pervasive influence. If richness of imagery, drawn as it is out of a clear perception of the rural landscape, could sustain a long poem, *The Shepherd's Calendar* would indeed be a classic.

But a poem requires form that emerges as effortlessly out of the material as Clare's imagery does. Too many of the "months" in this work lack that form. Storey has argued that *The Shepherd's Calendar* "is in many ways a test case for Clare's poetry. . . . For if his descriptive poetry is to be vindicated, it is in this work that we must seek that vindication."[17] A more appropriate place to look for Clare's best description contained in intricately wrought poems is in the sonnets and descriptive lyrics. This poem was Clare's major achievement to date, but he did not cease to develop his powers in 1823. The years that followed saw major developments and improvements in his technique without any diminution of his powers of perception.

IV   *1832 to 1841*

The period that began with his removal to Northborough in 1832 was one of continuous personal misfortune, but also of mature poetic accomplishment. It began in September with a proposal for publication of *The Midsummer Cushion,* the appearance of which was continually delayed to the detriment of Clare's financial situation and state of mind. Anxiety over his increasing debt and growing family led to a further deterioration of his health, which in turn resulted in his doctor's forbidding him to read or write in 1833. This situation was alleviated somewhat in the following year by payments for the copyright of what was now to be called *The Rural Muse* and by a gift from the Literary Fund. The publication of this volume in 1835 further restored Clare's peace of mind, but its failure with the public soon caused him more illness. His letters of the period contain several attempts to describe his illness to interested correspondents and to solicit their help in its treatment. As a result of these letters Dr. Darling prescribed an exercise in paraphrasing the

Psalms to help quiet his mind. Clare rigorously followed this advice—his manuscripts are filled with page after page of biblical paraphrase—but if it had any effect at all it was a temporary one and he was eventually taken, in June, 1837, to Dr. Matthew Allen's new asylum at High Beech, Essex. In his four years there his mind stabilized considerably and he continued to write poetry and read as many books as he could manage to borrow. His sense of isolation from home, both his real home with Patty and his imaginary one with the now-deceased Mary Joyce, permeates the poetry of the period, especially *Child Harold* and the songs, and eventually motivated his escape from High Beech in July, 1841. He composed a detailed prose account of his escape and several verse accounts of the disappointment he suffered on arrival at Northborough. He was allowed to remain at home until December of that year when he was taken to the Northampton General Lunatic Asylum for the remainder of his life.

Such a disastrous time in his personal life was accompanied by a period in his artistic life that produced the majority of his masterpieces. Some, like "[The Badger]," fall outside the scope of this chapter, but others, especially "Song's Eternity," reveal a new dimension in his treatment of experience and metaphor. He continued writing nature poems which, like "To the Nightingale," are rooted in a personal experience in the same way as those of the former period, and he began writing more and more songs which, though often traditional in both form and content, relied occasionally now and increasingly later on an inspirational experience similar to that which we have seen in his descriptive poems.

Like the poems of the previous period, but more polished in many respects, is "On Visiting a Favourite Place."[18] It opens with the memory of former pleasures, embodied in the symbol of Eden, that Clare enjoyed in the spot he is revisiting, and proceeds to bask in a corresponding pleasure in the present moment:

> There is a breath—indeed there is
> Of eden left—I feel it now
> Of somthing more then earthly bliss
> That falls and cheers my sullen brow.

He combines both his past and his present responses to the scene by stressing the escalating emotion that accompanies both and inspires him to preserve the experience in song:

> With verses dancing on my tongue
> The rapture of a heart at ease
> A fondness and a taste for song
> And love for places such as these
> A mind oerflowing with excess
> Of joys that spring from solitude
> That sees all nature spring to bless
> The heart away from noises rude
> So did its sunshine warm my brow
> And sure it gleams as lovely now.

The effect of solitude on the tranquil receptivity of a poet's mind soon produces overflowing emotions and the impulse to create poetry ("verses dancing on my tongue"). Similar references to various stages of the poetic process are dispersed throughout the poem, although they are not contained within a chronological narrative of rising feeling. The poem and the process, however, culminate in the final lines where Clare recalls the transformation of the scene that occurred during his former musings there:

> I viewed the trees and bushes near
> And distance till it grew to grey
> A power divine seemed everywhere
> And joys own rapture where I lay
> The furze clumps in their golden flowers
> Made edens in these golden hours.

Only now do we see the significance of Clare's recognizing an edenic atmosphere when he first returns to the scene in the opening lines; the "breath of eden" was created out of a previous transformation of the landscape by his poetic eye and now unites the two otherwise distinct experiences. And his memory of the conversion of furze clumps into types of Eden sparks the writing of the poem; it is the remarkable aspect of the scene from which he proceeds.

The whole poem is governed by this symbol; the innocent joy associated with Eden permeates Clare's response to the details he describes. And all these details are subordinated to his position in the landscape, all exist in the poem because of their influence on his state of mind. The trees and mole hills bid him welcome and the ant resents his presence, but none of the creatures or plants mentioned are superfluous. Apart from the simple personification throughout the poem, Clare's figurative language also demonstrates his growing ability to create metaphors out of his immediate surroundings. Unlike the rather awkward metaphor of the fishing rod in "Pastoral Fancies" the book metaphor here rises naturally out of Clare's personal experience:

> When last I paid a visit here
> The book I brought for leisures way
> Was useless for a volume dear
> In crowds of pictures round me lay
> The woods the heath the distant field
> In strips of green and russet dye
> Did such delicious pleasure yield
> I shut and put the volume bye
> The book at home was sweet indeed
> But there I felt I could not read.

If this is not yet the consummation of Clare's skill that we will see later in *Child Harold*, it is a measure of his advance over his earlier technique.

This progress is clearly marked in "What is There in the Distant Hills" and "Song's Eternity." In both poems Clare focuses as intently as he is able on the physical objects that surround him, in order to elicit from them an understanding of his own position in the natural scheme of things. Each derives its unity from the interrelationship between Clare's experience at the time he initially composes the poem and other experiences foreign both in time and place. From a fixed, rather than a rambling, point of view he ponders two sets of natural phenomena, producing poems reduced in the scale of their physical perceptions, but intensified in their vision. In the former he concentrates on his immediate location to examine the universal power of "the common things of everyday" to excite pleasure; in the latter he hears the sound of a bird singing *now* as a type of nature's continuous impulse toward song.

A series of questions and answers in "What is There in the Distant Hills"[19] illuminates one aspect of Clare's poetic creed. He places in opposition to the fens where he presently sits, the hills which he can only imagine:

> What is there in the distant hills
> My fancy longs to see
> That many a mood of joy instills
> Say what can fancy be
>
> Do old oaks thicken all the woods
> With weeds and brakes as here
> Does common water make the floods
> Thats common every where.

His continuation of this line of questioning for another five stanzas implies not an ignorance of the world outside North-borough so much as his suspicion that imagination tempts him to forsake his own response to nature for the mere sake of poetic fashion. He answers his own query with a conditional assessment of the conflict within his mind:

> If so my fancy idly clings
> To notions far away
> And longs to roam for common things
> All round her every day
>
> Right idle would the journey be
> To leave ones home so far
> And see the moon I now can see
> And every little star.

Concluding that a lust for novelty is misleading because he already has the material for poetic pleasure *here*, he argues himself out of the urge to roam. His immediate response to the scene before him, in this spot, embodies what is lasting in human experience; his dissatisfaction with ordinary nature is—he repeats the word—idle. As if incredulous, though, he resumes his questioning by citing the example of the moon which embraces both his present situation and that of others in various parts of the world. Having considered that example, he seems convinced of the validity of his views on nature as an inspiration for poetry:

> The poets in the tales they tell
> And with their happy powers
> Have made lands where their fancys dwell
> Seem better lands than ours
>
> Their storied woods and vales and streams
> Grow up within the mind
> Like beauty seen in pleasant dreams
> We no where else can find.
>
> Yet common things no matter what
> Which nature dignifyes
> If happ[i]ness be in their lot
> They gratify our eyes.

More confident now than in his earlier answer that the touchstone of true poetry is fidelity to personal experience in nature, he verifies that assertion by examining his immediate surroundings. He finds them capable of producing all the pleasure he can imagine:

> This moss upon the sallow roots
> Of this secluded spot
> Finds seasons that its [temper] suits
> And blossoms unforgot
>
> Why need I sigh for hills to see
> If grass be their array
> While here the little paths go through
> The grasses every day
>
> Such fancy fills the restless mind
> At once to cheat and cheer
> With thought and zemblance undefined
> No where and everywhere.

Asserting the value of the individual, present experience as a basis for poetic interpretation of nature, he also implies that it contains the essence of all other experiences; that reliance on imaginary responses to nature only takes us further from a true insight into our environment. The geographical dichotomy between the hills and the fens, the "here" and the "there," is particularly appropriate.

It not only works on a physical and metaphorical level in this poem; it also tells us something about Clare's maturity as a nature poet. His own development corresponds to his increasing tendency to root his poems in the "here," rejecting the exotic subject in favor of a unique response to what is common— rejecting, in his words, the "nowhere" for the "everywhere." The fact that he supports his argument by pointing out the example of "this secluded spot" demonstrates how he has learned to eliminate extraneous elements in favor of a clear, intense look at a particular scene. Thus a "restless mind" tempts the poet to create artificial poetic experiences, and is opposed to that "easy thoughtlessness of thought" which enables the poet's eye to transform ordinary nature into a source of pleasure and, eventually, into a work of art. The lesson he learns from contemplating this spot brings the inevitable ecstasy of Clare's poetic process:

> O natures pleasant moods and dreams
> In every journey lies
> That glads my heart with simple themes
> And cheers and gratifyes.

Had Clare finished with this climax his poem would have had more force; the two succeeding stanzas are a blemish not, perhaps, for anything they say, but for the verse in which they are phrased. The conclusion notwithstanding, "What is There in the Distant Hills" is a concentrated work which overcomes Clare's earlier propensity to ramble both in his contact with nature and, more dangerously for his poetry, in his organization of those experiences into poems.

"Song's Eternity"[20] carries Clare's intensification a step further by inviting the reader to share his insight and by attempting to re-create the ecstasy of his experience in the reader. The entire thematic statement of the poem emerges from the physical situation to which he draws our attention in the opening stanza:

> What is songs eternity
> Come and see
> Can it noise and bustle be
> Come and see

> Praises sung or praises said
> Can it be
> Wait awhile and these are dead
> Sigh sigh
> Be they high or lowly bred
> They die.

To answer his initial question Clare simply points verbally to a bird's demonstration of the continuity of song. His own response to the bird becomes a symbol which embodies several aspects of the answer he is to explore in the remainder of the poem, aspects such as the momentary vitality and eternal recurrence of natural song. The experience is a simple one, described only briefly in the fourth stanza:

> Dreamers list the honey be
> Mark the tree,
> Where the blue cap tootle tee
> Sings a glee
> Sung to adam and to eve—
> Here they be.

But from this contemplation of an ordinary bird's song, the "here" and "now" of the poem, Clare makes profound implications about the "then" and "there." He hears in this scene an embodiment of the same harmony between man and his environment that characterized prelapsarian existence, a harmony unaffected by the transience of the "crowds and cities" of human civilization and unaltered by the wrath of God manifest in the flood:

> When floods covered every bough
> Noahs ark
> Heard that ballad singing now
> Hark hark.

In other words, the present experience is a universal one which contains within it the essence of melodies in different locations both geographical and chronological. Thus to the question "mighty songs that miss decay, / what are they?" Clare can point to this bird singing as a demonstration of the answer because, as

he says in a stanza from another manuscript but obviously
intended to form part of this poem,

> The eternity of song
>   Liveth here
> Natures universal tongue
>   Singeth here
> Songs I heard and felt and seen
>   Everywhere
> Songs like the grass are evergreen
>   The giver
> Said live and be and they have been
>   For ever.

The emphatic repetition of "here" indicates how important his
immediate situation is. He has moved beyond the comparison of
metaphor to the use of an experience that is not simply an
illustration but an embodiment of the abstract concept of eternal
song. By simply pointing to the symbol he achieves the ultimate
reduction of poetic interpretation. Nature speaks for herself with
a minimum of distortion from the poet's voice.

Clare's versification supports his faith in the symbol. Through
his unabashed repetition of rhyming long vowels, brought close
together by the shortness of the lines which contain them, he
successfully transfers the music he is talking about into the sound
of the poem. He establishes a melody in his verse which
constantly reminds us that he is writing about music. He goes one
step further in his aural reproduction of the sound of birds' songs,
trying to convey as directly as possible not only the concept of
music but the sound of the specific music he hears. Risking the
appearance of simplicity or naïveté he incorporates the
bluecap's sound into his verse:

> Tootle tootle tootle tee
> Can it be
> Pride and fame must shadows be
> Come and see.

The distillation of a message out of nature by allowing nature to
speak for herself represents the end for which his poetic method
strove. No longer bringing in a plethora of extraneous sights and
sounds, he now excludes all but the most pertinent details.

It is hard to envisage a poem more successful than this in justifying Clare's theory of the poet's responsibility to nature. He not only preserves the sound of the bird's song, but reminds us of its context in the yearly cycle of seasons, the biblical origins of man, and the rise and fall of civilizations. With his childlike clarity of vision, expressed through simple lyrics, he conveys an elemental understanding of nature and poetry. To Clare, the impulse to sing is as integral a part of nature as the color of grass—as the movement of the spheres themselves—and requires for its understanding only a natural response to its manifestation in a bird's song. His listening to the bird sing is an example of man's ability to experience the eternal, to participate in a natural pleasure that predates his own history.

V   *1842 to 1864*

During the last period of his life, spent in the asylum at Northampton, Clare writes less frequently of his individual response to nature. When he does it is either to mourn his loss of contact with it or to use it as an objective correlative to his other emotional experiences. The bulk of his work written between 1842 and his death in 1864 consists of songs, and most of his descriptions of nature are adapted to the requirements of that subgenre. Clare seems to have been unable, or unwilling, to sustain the experimentation with experience and metaphor which reached its zenith in his High Beech days, possibly because of his increasingly disturbed mind which was obviously capable of fine outbursts of song and poetry, but not of consistent development in his art. He left incomplete his two ambitious works of 1841, *Child Harold* and *Don Juan,* and confined himself to short poems for the rest of his life. But a more likely reason for his decline in experimentation with the kind of poem we have been discussing stems from his being allowed less frequent rambles outside the asylum walls, hence fewer poetic experiences upon which to base his poems. As a result, he wrote made-to-order love songs and several poems from former, remembered experiences, as well as sea songs and drinking songs that have not yet been published. The few poems in which he does employ personal experiences use them very simply, with none of the complexity or subtlety of his best previous ones.

The most common technique of these few poems is to describe the poet's surroundings as a prelude to his praise of a woman. The love songs which result often carry little authentic emotion, but some of them contain their own charm and a few, like "The Winds Blow Softly" and "The Sweetest Woman There," reveal an effective blending of natural description and conventional passion. This second poem begins by defining the present time and conveying a sense of gloom through description of the landscape:

> From bank to bank the water roars Like thunder in a storm
> A Sea in sight of both the shores Creating no alarm
> The water birds above the flood fly o'er the foam and spray
> And nature wears a gloomy hood on this October day.[21]

Clare justifies his introduction of the woman in the next stanza by viewing her in the context of his past experiences in the same location:

> And there I saw a bonny maid That proved my hearts delight
> All day she was a Goddess made An angel fair at night
> We loved and in each others power Felt nothing to condemn
> I was the leaf and she the flower And both grew on one stem.

Note here how the metaphors are created from the natural objects in the scene and the woman's form, becoming in the last two lines the vehicle for describing the intimacy of their relationship. Clare follows this stanza with mention of the change she causes in his view of the landscape. By incorporating her presence into the scene he enhances both his memory of her and his present view of his surroundings:

> I loved her lip her cheek her eye She cheered my midnight gloom
> A bonny rose neath Gods own sky in one perennial bloom
> She lives mid pastures evergreen And meadows ever fair
> Each winter spring and summer scene The sweetest woman there.

He concludes the poem by correlating her beauty with nature's and the depressing opening description with his particular sentiment for the woman. He speaks of her power to transform the lonely landscape in the past tense, accenting the effect of her present absence:

She lives among the meadow floods That foams and roars away
While fading hedgerows distant woods Fade off to naked spray
She lives to cherish and delight All nature with her face
She brought me joy morn noon and night In that low lonely place.

The progress of the experience and the description of the situation are simple but effective, and they add an element of sophistication to what would otherwise be another nondescript love song. The lengths to which he carries this technique in other songs we will explore in a later chapter.

But perhaps the finest poem of this period to create its imagery out of the poet's immediate experience is "Clifford Hill":

> The river rambles like a snake
>   Along the meadow green
> And loud the noise the mill wheels make
>   I' summer time at e'en
> And there as swift the waters pass
>   So runs the life of man
> I sit me down upon the grass
>   These beauties for to scan
>
> Tis summers day and dewy eve
>   And sweet the sun sinks low
> I smile and yet my heart will greive
>   To see the waters flow
> To see the flags that look so green
>   The sun gilt waves so bright
> I wander here this lovely e'en
>   In wonder and delight
>
> The firs look dark on Clifford's hill
>   The river bright below
> All foamed beneath the water mill
>   While beautious flowers do blow
> Tis here I'd wander morn and night
>   With fondly gazing eye
> To see the sunny golden light
>   Go down in yonder sky—
>
> Yes dearly do these scenes I love
>   And dear that fir clad hill

> There all secure does build the dove
>   While click-clack goes the mill
> And now in natures sweet repose
>   I leave this spot awile;
> The bee is buried in the rose
>   And man gone from his toil.[22]

The river, identified in the opening stanza as a metaphor for the passing life of man, dominates the remainder of the poem and explains the curiously mixed emotions the poet acknowledges in the second stanza. The tension between the fullness of summer and the sinking sensation that accompanies the setting sun corresponds with the poet's paradoxical admission that "I smile, and yet my heart will greive." Looking at the river, hearing the mill's audible reminder that the water is flowing, and associating both in his mind with the passing of life, he cannot miss the implications of transience which alloy his momentary enjoyment of the scene. Other details reinforce the paradox; the dark firs form a constrast to the bright river and the measured passing of the water is quietly ignored by the dove preparing for the future. All these images emerge directly from the description and continue to work throughout the poem without overtly reminding us of their significance.

Success like this was not often achieved in the type of poem we are concerned with, however. The final period of his life was one not of triumph but decline. He turned his mind to other types of poetry, pausing only now and then for outbursts of nature-inspired enthusiasm which indicate the reawakening of the poetic impulse:

> How beautiful is Sunset
>   eye and breast
> Is filled with extacys
>   of love and joy
>
> The georgius liver
>   the glorious west
> Is one short glance of
>   heaven from the Sky.[23]

Most of Clare's life at Northampton was uneventful save for his fortunate contact with W. F. Knight, who collected and transcribed most of the poems, and Clare's employment at helping Anne Elizabeth Baker compile her *Glossary of North-ampton Words and Phrases*. In the early spring of 1864 he wrote his last poem, "Bird's Nests," and on May 20 of that year he died peacefully at the asylum.

His achievement is considerable and this chapter has dealt with only a limited part of it. But even the development we have seen reveals his experimentation to control and record the mental excitement he experienced during the poetic process. The sonnets, most of the songs, and *Child Harold* demand separate treatment, since their appeal lies in a fully consum-mated impression rather than the demonstration of a developing form.

CHAPTER 4

The Sonnets

CLARE was writing sonnets as early as his fourteenth or fifteenth year, having composed his first after "seeing two very pretty ones in an old newspaper I think they were by Charlotte Smith."[1] He continued to write in this form well into his later life at the Northampton Asylum, experimenting with various standard types, but eventually developing a distinct style of his own. Although he has left few personal remarks in his letters and prose from which we could deduce his theory of sonnet writing, one poem credits that form with nursing his confidence in poetry to the point where he was able to branch out into more ambitious forms:

> I walked with poesy in the sonnets bounds
> With little hopes yet many a wild delight
> As timid childern take their summer rounds
> And scarce dare leave their cottage out of sight
> Till field and meadow and the summer light
> Tempteth them farther with their fears to roam
> So from the sonnets little garden home
> I went sweet natures wilderness to trace.[2]

We may doubt the accuracy of this version of his development as a poet — he was writing "Helpston which [he] intended for a long poem in the manner of Goldsmith" and "The Fate of Amy," another long poem, at the time of composing his earliest surviving sonnets[3] — but we can be sure that much of his early experimentation in poetry focused on the possibilities offered by that form. If his prose reveals little evidence of his thoughts on the sonnet, the poems themselves indicate a mind exploring its potential, seeking new variations of the traditional forms which would suit the modern subject of landscape description which was his forte.

This experimentation must be stressed. In their influential biography of Clare the Tibbles have fostered the misconception that Clare "knew nothing of octave and sestet, and only a little about presentation and application of idea, pause and continuity."[4] They emphasize the individuality of Clare's later sonnets, but by ignoring his initial efforts to adapt traditional techniques to his own purposes they not only disregard a great deal of Clare's poetic output, but undermine the significant origins of his later work. Perhaps they have taken too literally Clare's modest disclaimer in a note to Rev. Isaiah Holland accompanying some of his sonnets: "You perceive I take little Notice of the Mechanism which all Sonneteers in general are particular to Notice — They are the Wild notes of a Labour[er] & the unpolishd heartfelt feelings of a Lowly Clown who is not acquainted with the craft and Subtlety of Art to make them agreeable to the tastfull Eye."[5] We know from other letters and his journal that Clare read widely in the sonnets of earlier centuries because he mentions not only those of Shakespeare, "which are great favorites of mine," but Milton's sonnet on his blindness, and his acquaintance with Drayton, Spenser, and Surrey as well.[6] It is surprising, perhaps, that he never wrote love sonnets to his idealized Mary Joyce in the way Petrarch did to his Madonna Laura, or Sidney to Penelope Devereux, or Shakespeare to his dark lady, but it was not unusual that he should notice the structural devices employed by these previous writers.

A glance at his surviving manuscripts indicates just how concerned Clare was with octave and sestet, with the formal arrangement of ideas which the sonnet required, and with the need to make the appearance of structure correspond with the inner form of his subject. An early poem which Clare reworked several times before including it in *Poems Descriptive of Rural Life and Scenery* will serve as an example. It appears in two early manuscripts under the title "Sonnet, on the Pismire":

> Thou little insect, infinitely small,
>> What curious texture, marks thy minute frame,
> How seeming large thy foresight, and withall,
>> Thy labouring tallents, not unworthy fame!

> To raise, such monstrous hills, along the plain,
>   Largher than mountains, when compar'd with thee!
> To drag the crumb, dropt by the village swain,
>   Thrice bigger than thy self,—is strange, indeed to me.
>
> But that great instinct, which foretells the cold,
>   And bids 'em gard, 'gainst winters, wasteful power,
> Endues this mite, with cheerfulnes to hold,
>   Her toiling labours, thro the sultry hour.
>
> So that same soothing power, or Misery,
> Cheers the poor Pilghrim, to Eternity!![7]

Here the subject is divided on the page into three distinct quatrains, the first outlining the general characteristics of the pismire, the second featuring his physical strength and stamina as referred to in the first quatrain, and the third concentrating on his most unique quality—instinct. The final couplet draws a parallel between the natural instinct of the ant and the faith of the Christian soul. Although the sonnet is not a particularly effective one, the second quatrain having little to do with the comparison illustrated in the third quatrain and the couplet, the poem demonstrates a young poet coming to terms with the sonnet structure by visualizing it on the page in separate structural units.

When Clare copied the poem into a later notebook he retitled it "The Ant" and merged the first two quatrains into an octave, perhaps realizing that the second quatrain was more appropriately an extension of the last line of the first quatrain than a complete subject in itself.[8] Consequently, the exclamation mark after "fame" was changed to a semicolon and a dash, weakening the division between the quatrains. This punctuation is further diminished to a comma in the first printed version of the poem and the spatial divisions are, as usual in printed sonnets, eliminated. The period after the octave marks the only firm division in the final appearance of the poem. Gradually Clare's divisions have disappeared in the visual sense, but the more important distinction between units of subject matter and their interrelationship is no less apparent in Tibble's printing of the poem than in its original manuscript form.

The clear divisions between units of the sonnet in this poem are typical of numerous other poems in the manuscripts. In "The

Moon," for example, the sestet contains a description of the qualities of the moon while the octave, separated by a space on the page, relates those characteristics to the Christian life. In "Evening" the opening quatrain is followed by an octave and a couplet, all of which are separated by a physical space as well as by their subject matter. And in "The Glow-worm" the final couplet is separated from the preceding twelve lines which are in turn broken into quatrain and octave, not, this time, by a space but by a period, the octave itself being one continuous statement.[9]

This variety of relationships between internal units of the sonnet form illustrates Clare's search for an assimilation of form and content in his early work. The search led him to several unorthodox experiments which, although they failed to produce great poems initially, eventually contributed to the development of his own individual type of sonnet. He occasionally tried a series of seven couplets, for instance, and even seems to have considered a twelve-line poem in one of his notebooks to be a sonnet, since it appears to be complete in itself and is entitled simply "Sonnet." At least one other sonnet, "The Landscip," he divided into a quatrain, a seven-line unit, and a tercet.[10] Perhaps the most startling of these early experiments, though, was his shifting of the couplet from its accustomed position as an epigrammatical conclusion, to an equally emphatic location elsewhere in the poem. This was to be a favorite device later, but even in the early manuscripts such poems as "Christian Faith" contain this innovation.[11]

The result of all his experimentation was a group of early sonnets primarily derivative, but seldom indentical to traditional forms, and another, smaller, group stamped with Clare's original style.

I *The Early Experiments*

On February 21, 1822, Clare admitted to John Taylor, "I have written no sonnets lately—I am sick of the short winded pevishness that hovers round this 14 line article in poetry."[12] By the next January he felt little more inclined to write, as he told James Hessey: "I have not written a song since I left you & it is months now since I even scribbld a Sonnet."[13] This dissatisfaction with the form had evaporated by January, 1824, however—

perhaps because the rest from such composition gave him time to
sort out his own views on the sonnet. At any rate, he found
himself in that month contemplating a new start, one that would
break him free of the fetters of tradition that had bound his
attempts to that date: "I have made it up in my mind to write one
hundred Sonnets as a set of pictures on the scenes of objects that
appear in the different seasons & as I shall do it soly for
amusement I shall take up wi gentle & simple as they come
whatever in my eye finds any interest not merely in the view for
publication but for attempts."[14] This statement explains the large
number of inferior works among the sonnets Clare wrote; he was
not above making an "attempt" for no other purpose than to see
whether it would work. He is warning us against looking for
polished sonnets in each fourteen-line poem we find in his
manuscripts; many were not intended for print. But he is also
giving us an indication of the direction he intended to pursue. No
longer concerned, as he so often was in the years up to 1824, to
inject an element of meditation or personal observation to
legitimize his response to nature, he proposes a set of pictures for
his own amusement, pictures that will correspond to his true
reaction to nature and not to the one he felt was demanded by
the reading public. The result was a period of high achievement
in his chosen form, a period that defined his new view of the
sonnet and produced his best fourteen-line poems.

In the years before this new inspiration came, however, Clare
had written several competent sonnets, some mere reflective
poems, but others, like "The Setting Sun," combining the
eighteenth-century preference for meditation with his own
peculiar response to nature. The octave in this poem establishes
the poet's situation and hints, especially in the ambivalent use of
"heavenly," at the lesson he is to draw from the scene he
contemplates:

> This scene how beautious to the musing mind
> That now swift slides from my enchanting view
> The Sun sweet setting yon far hills behind
> In other worlds his visits to renew
> What spangling glories all around him shine
> What nameless colours cloudles and serene
> (A heavenly prospect brightest in decline)
> Attend his exit from this lovly scene.[15]

He dwells on the movement he experiences, the scene "sliding" from his view as the light fades and the sun moving on to other scenes in distant places. In most manuscript versions this process of change is further emphasized by the use of the present, active "enchanting" and "spangling" where Tibble inexplicably prints the past, static "enchanted" and "spangled."[16] The important element of the scene is the phenomenon of the sun appearing "brightest in decline," gaining intensity from being perceived at the precise moment it begins to disappear. Clare makes that element of the scene the basis for his moral in the sestet:

> —So sets the christians sun in glories clear
> So shines his soul at his departure here
> No clouding doubts nor misty fears arise
> To dim hopes golden rays of being forgiven
> His sun sweet setting in the clearest skyes
> In safe assurance wings the soul to heaven.

To mark the importance of the parallel between the two sections of the poem, Clare again moves the couplet to the point of nearest contact between them. The remainder of the sestet merely elaborates the point made in the couplet. Clare sees the Christian soul at its strongest when it seems to be waning; at the point where physical death seems to be overcoming it it is in fact preparing for its exit from life, but also its movement on to the ultimate experience in heaven. The message of this poem is not a result of an intensely personal insight into the nature of the universe; rather it indicates Clare's propensity in these early sonnets to imitate his inferiors and to write the kind of poetry he thought would sell. His own views on religion, although he seems to have flirted with the organized church during occasional bouts of depression, were not in conflict with his sentiments here, but they lacked the tight orthodoxy implied in the poem: "my creed may be different from other creeds but the difference is nothing when the end is the same—if I did not expect & hope for eternal happiness I should be ever miserable & as every religion is a rule leading to good by its professor the religions of all nations & creeds where that end is the aim ought rather to be respected than scoffed at."[17] Many of his own early sonnets, however, contain pious platitudes of orthodox Christianity like this in "The Setting Sun." Only in the asylum poems do we get his real creed

distilled from his personal experience of life. But even in this
early poem he has suffered from editorial emendations which
have replaced in Tibble's publication his original "safe
assurance" in the last line with a more orthodox "faith's
assurance."

A few of the early sonnets prefigure Clare's later, more
mature, view of the themes and techniques appropriate to the
form. In some of them he begins to utilize the limited space of
the sonnet to capture precise moments of time which, because of
their brevity, require a short form of expression. He also
recognizes that the emotional complexity they inspire demands a
form that imposes a structural clarity on the poet's response.
Thus we see him wrestling with the problem of perception and
expression in "Written in Autumn":

> Checkt autumn doubly sweet is thy declining
> To meditate thee in this wilderd shade
> To view the wood in its pied lustre shining
> And catch each varied beauty as they fade
> Where oer broad hazel leaves thy pencil mellows
> Red as the glow that mornings opening warms
> And as[h] and maple neath thy color yellows
> As robd some sunbeam of its setting charms
> O Id say much of what now meets my eye
> But beautys loose me in variety
> O for the warmth of soul and witching measure
> Of 'xpressive zemblance poesy which is thine
> And genius eye to view this transient treasure
> That autumn here might lastingly decline.[18]

This poem is concerned not with the task of abstracting morals
out of the landscape, but with the more basic and more difficult
problem of expressing the precise nature of the landscape at the
exact moment of perception. The sonnet, like a picture, provides
a means of capturing a scene from out of the continuum of time,
motion, and change. But, unlike the picture, the sonnet is an art
form which unfolds only in time, the time required to read it, and
time which is itself relatively limited by the conventional length
of the sonnet. Therefore, Clare attempts to "catch each varied
beauty as they fade"—to capture the essence of the season's
change by evoking something of that process in his poetry. He

calls on the muse to assist him in making autumn "lastingly decline."

In a limited sense, however, he has already achieved this. The first eight lines have not only listed the elements of the scene that contribute to the sense of decline, but have arranged them in such a way that we are drawn through them in a continuous movement, reaching no pause that resembles a full stop until the tenth line. Clare has attempted in the octave a formal correlation between the subject and the form. In the couplet he switches the subject to the difficulty that such correlation involves, by stating the problem directly: "O Id say much of what now meets my eye / But beautys loose me in variety." He is not yet master of his technique, not yet capable of producing a satisfactory impression of the emotional response provoked by the scene of change. He is asking the poem to achieve what nature cannot—the extended decline, the preservation of the actual experience of waning life—by savoring the precise moment of change in the landscape. There is no fear of change here as is so often alleged against Clare; he savors it, desiring to prolong the experience in his verse.

The role of the season in this poem, as an artist wielding a "pencil mellow" to transform an ordinary scene into a rich experience, was to have an important place in Clare's subsequent poetry. Hence the emphasis on color, where it indicates the variety of beauty at this time of year, also illustrates the change Clare is writing about. Each hue is a manifestation of a precise point in the process of decline which accompanies autumn. This function of the artist recurs frequently in the sonnets, and in many of the longer poems too, often as a season, but usually as the wind in close alliance with a specific time of the year. "Summer Tints," for example, treats a similar theme to that of "Written in Autumn," although without the appeal to the powers of poetry:

> How sweet Ive wanderd bosom deep in grain
> When summers mellowing pencil sweeps his shades
> Of ripening tinges oer the checkerd plain
> Light tawny oat lands wi their yellow blades
> And bearded corn like armys on parade
> Beans lightly scorchd that still preservd their green

And nodding lands of wheat in bleachy brown
And streaking banks where many a maid and clown
Contrasts a sweetness to the rural scene
Forming the little haycocks up and down
While oer the face of nature softly swept
The lingering wind mixing the brown and green
So sweet that shepherds from their bowers have crept
And stood delighted musing oer the scene.[19]

Both summer and the wind have artistic powers, the season
shading the landscape and the wind blending the colors. This is
only one of numerous sonnets that contradict Thomas Frosch's
contention that "the wind usually appears in [Clare's] landscape
as a signal of loss; it is an emblem of the imminent destruction
that almost always contextualizes his visions of happy scenes."[20]
On the contrary, the wind is responsible in most of these poems
for the "breathing hues" that Clare favored in Peter DeWint's
landscape paintings and drawings.

Clare's own words provide the best explanation of the role
wind played in his perception of landscape:

Hail, gentle winds! I love your murmuring sounds,
The willows charm me wavering to and fro;
And oft I stretch me on the daisied ground,
To see you crimp the wrinkled flood below:
Delighted more as brisker gusts succeed,
And give the landscape round a sweeter grace,
Sweeping in shaded waves the rip'ning mead,
Puffing their rifled fragrance in my face.
Pictures of nature! ye are doubly dear,
Her children dearly love your whispering charms;
Ah, ye have murmur'd sweet to many an ear
That now lies dormant in deaths icy arms;
And at this moment many a weed ye wave,
That hides the bard in his forgotten grave.[21]

The motion of the wind is the single important element in the
scene, progressing from "gentle" to "brisker" to "puffing," and
evoking in the poet a correspondingly deeper emotion. The wind
again creates a "picture" of nature and its activity continues after
that of the poet has passed away. What appears to be a rather
abrupt change of subject in the final couplet is in fact an
extension of the scene previously described. The poet has moved

from one prone position in the landscape—"oft I stretch me on the daisied ground"—to the ultimate physical union with it in death. His personal relationship to the landscape, and especially to the wind, is only an extension of that of other poets who have responded to the sound of the wind. The sensual quality of this sonnet is not as evocative as in "Written in Autumn" or "Summer Tints," but it is more complex. It is visually present in the "wrinkled" water and the "shaded waves" of the meadow, but it is also olfactory in the "rifled fragrance," an effective phrase describing the wind's possession of what appears to be, but is not, its own scent. Furthermore, the wind is responsible for the auditory appeal that similar landscapes have made to the now-dead poets.

Many of the sonnets of this period are indirectly about the process of artistic, especially literary, creation, but at least one deals with the subject directly. In "Expression" Clare examines the conflict between the mysterious power of creation which he experienced when composing his verse, and the rather mundane subjects which he felt were appropriate to poetry. The poem is divided into two seven-line sections, the first outlining the creative urge:

> Expression throbbing utterance of the soul
> Born when some frenzied bard his muses fires
> Bursts oer his feelings in un awd controul
> And up to heavens top most height aspires
> Stealing the music of some angels song
> To tell of all he sees and all admires
> Which fancys colours paint so sweet so strong.[22]

This is the aesthetic mysticism we are accustomed to find in Clare's asylum poetry. Its compelling verse suggests the urgent movement of mental excitation which accompanies the process of poetic composition. The verse moves with consummate immediacy through a series of plosives which demonstrate, almost physically, the poet's bursting emotion, until both verse and emotion reach their climax at the end of the fourth line. Subsequently, the subordinate clauses fall away one after another in explanation of the more fanciful ideas in the opening lines. The conflict between subject and expression surfaces in the word "un awd." Clare's own awe at the power of expression invests this word with a special significance. He seems surprised that poets in the ecstasy of composition are not overawed by the power they possess, that the impulse toward expression overcomes the natural temerity of poets like Clare. The second half of the poem outlines the modest material Clare favored for his own poetry:

> And to far humbler scenes thou dost belong
> In sorrow thou art warm when speaking tears
> Down some sad cheek in silence wail their wrong
> And ah most sweet expression sweet appears
> Thy smiles of gratitude whose bosoms bleed
> Tho high the lofty poets frenzy steers
> In natures simplest garb thourt sweet indeed.

The mundane verse of this half of the poem, when compared to the enthusiasm of the first, indicates which aspect of his subject inspired Clare most. He recognized a need to draw his inspiration from the rural peasant life around him, but he achieved a full poetic experience only when that material caught fire, inexplicably, in his imagination.

Two other sonnets deserve mention before we move on to Clare's more mature works in the genre: "The Arbour" because it demonstrates the individual view of his subject which Clare was gradually developing, and "Evening Primrose" because it is an effective example of how unconventional Clare was willing to be in his versification. The subject of "The Arbour" is a typical Romantic one, a grove of trees which—often in Wordsworth and Coleridge, but at times in Clare too—was celebrated as a place of solitude and peace, or of shelter from the physical elements. Clare's view here is different:

> There is a wilderd spot delights me well
> Pent in a corner of my native vale
> Where tiney blossoms with a purple bell
> Shivers their beauties to the autumn gale
> Tis one of those mean arbours that prevail
> With manhoods weakness still to seek and love
> For what is past—destructions axe did fail
> To maul it down with its companion grove
> Tho but a trifling thorn oft sheltering warm
> A brood of summer birds by nature led

> To seek for covert in a hasty storm
> I often think it lifts its lonley cares
> In piteous bloom where all the rest is fled
> Like a poor warrior the rude battle spares.[23]

Clare's arbor is exposed, capable of protecting birds, but more fascinating to the poet for its own vulnerability, depending only on the whims of man for its continued existence. But it has a kind of dignity, too. It has survived not because it is a thing of beauty, but because it appeals to man's sense of propriety, his instinctive acknowledgment that natural objects deserve to live because they have formed part of our past experience. Clare's picture of the arbor is conveyed in a single, controlled description with no extraneous elements. And it is clinched by an effective metaphor in the concluding line. The dignity of a war-scarred, tattered soldier is appropriate not only in a visual sense, but also for the human element that threatens to break through the description from the beginning. Clare was himself one of those who relied on the indulgence of others for his livelihood and his place in literary society. His intrinsic literary merit was not always sufficiently obvious to contemporary tastes to prevent that dependence. That is not to say "The Arbour" is a poem about Clare's personal predicament; it is only to point out his propensity to identify with natural objects, like the thorn, whose situation said something about his own. He is a kindred spirit here, as he was to be in numerous other, sometimes better, poems.

The iambic tetrameter couplets of "Evening Primrose," by moving the rhymes into closer proximity with each other than the normal pentameter alternating rhymes, give the impression of sounds dropping gently and frequently on the ear. The first six lines effectively delay the introduction of the flower while they establish the atmosphere within which it flourishes:

> When once the sun sinks in the west
> And dew drops pearl the evenings breast
> Almost as pale as moonbeams are
> Or its companionable star
> The Evening Primrose opes anew
> Its delicate blossoms to the dew.[24]

Clare's diction was not always as pure as this in the early years of
his composition, but when it was he could find such appropriate,
yet unobtrusive, verbs as "pearl" to carry the precise meaning he
was after. The remainder of this poem employs a similar restraint
and economy to suggest the delicate personality of the flower:

> And shunning hermit of the light
> Wastes its fair bloom upon the night
> Who blindfold to its fond caresses
> Knows not the beauty it posseses
> Thus it blooms on till night is bye
> And day looks out with open eye
> Bashed at the gaze it cannot shun
> It faints and withers and is done.

It shuns the light, but remains unappreciated by the darkness to
which it belongs. Again we cannot help feeling that Clare's
identification with the flower in the last couplet, an almost
prophetic picture of his eventual fate, was perhaps one of his
early premonitions of what his exposure to the public gaze would
lead to. Even without our knowledge of his subsequent
biography, however, this is a suggestive poem, creating a
relationship between the primrose and the night reminiscent of
Blake's rose and worm, with the same assurance that the
universal implications of a simple analogy will be caught by the
reader. Only the slightest touch of personification is sufficient to
elevate Clare's vision of a flower to the sphere of human
significance. Like Blake's poem, "Evening Primrose" conveys the
poignancy of human betrayal and the inevitable, even natural,
opposition of beauty and destruction in this world.

II *The Mature Accomplishment*

Clare's renewed interest in the sonnet after 1824 produced a
revised concept of the form, based, it is true, on his earlier
experiments, but possessing a new vitality and added maturity.
He no longer relies so heavily on drawing morals from his
observations of nature, feeling more confident in his simple
expressions of emotional response to what he sees, and concentrating more on creating an evocative picture of the
landscape. As a result, he less often divides his sonnets into

traditional divisions, replacing octave and sestet with continuously flowing verse which uses the total fourteen lines as its boundary. In this innovation he was deriving his form directly from the subject matter that more and more preoccupied him, the concept of time in its relationship to the experience of reading a poem. He also explored the possibility of capturing a specific moment of time in his verse, demonstrating for the first time an interest in moments of mystical vision and the feelings of rapture that he experienced in the process of poetic composition. Among all these new starts, on the other hand, were numerous forms as derivative as his earlier sonnets, and even more extensive "attempts"—experiments with ideas and forms which resulted in no further development, presumably because Clare could see no place to extend that particular innovation.

Perhaps the most immediately noticeable of these innovations was Clare's utilization of the full fourteen lines of the sonnet as an indivisible poetic unit. More and more frequently he was attempting to describe a single reaction to a unified scene without further division into sections. At the same time he was dropping the didactic element which required its own segment of the poem to make clear its application to the description. A good example of the direction he was taking is "The Foddering Boy":

> The foddering boy along the crumping snows
> With straw band belted legs and folded arm
> Hastens and on the blast that keenly blows
> Oft turns for breath and beats his fingers warm
> And shakes the lodging snows from off his cloaths
> Buttoning his doublet closer from the storm
> And slouching his brown beaver oer his nose
> Then faces it agen—and seeks the stack
> Within its circling fence—were hungry lows
> Expecting cattle making many a track
> About the snows—impatient for the sound
> When in hugh fork fulls trailing at his back
> He litters the sweet hay about the ground
> And brawls to call the staring cattle round.[25]

Not only is the scene a unified picture without the author's commentary, it is described in a single continuous movement of coordinate and subordinate clauses. Clare's technique becomes particularly impressive if we look closely at the way he suggests activity outside his frame without violating the unity of the picture within it. The chronological point at which the poet views the scene is defined in line eight where the boy is in the act of seeking the haystack; the action that follows is merely anticipated. The cattle are expecting a future action, they are "impatient for the sound / *when*" he will litter the ground with their fodder (italics mine). Thus a single act provides the focus, but implicit in that act is the action that will inevitably follow, beyond the moment captured in the sonnet. Clare's diction further merges the present with the future: by using the future "when" in conjunction with the present "litters" the proposed littering of the ground gives the impression of happening immediately. Thus within the sonnet we have an actual and an implied description molded into a single scene. In addition there is no didactic intrusion by the poet; we sense his sympathetic response to what he sees, but he remains outside the scene, content to let the description itself convey his attitude.

Accompanying this break from the traditional structure of the sonnet was Clare's developing skill in manipulating a continuous movement of verse from beginning to end of the fourteen lines. This skill came in response to his treatment of the captured moment with which we have seen him experimenting in the earlier sonnets. Usually that moment contained its own transience, the setting sun at its peak of beauty or the wind's motion as it blended colors into a kinesthetic picture. To capture the true character of that moment, therefore, Clare needed a technique to convey the feeling of motion in his verse. And to give the sense of this motion happening instantaneously he chose the brief form of the sonnet without any further division into subordinate units. He learned, in short, to manipulate the speed at which the sonnet was read. And it is this quality of his sonnets that distinguishes them from the photographer's or the painter's art, or from the "verbal equivalent for the small woodcut so brilliantly practised by Bewick."[26] Something of the difference can be seen in the first eight lines of "June":

> Go where I will nought but delight is seen
> The blue and luscious sky is one broad gleam
> Of universal extacy—the green

> Rich sweeping meadow and the laughing stream
> As sweet as happiness on heavens breast
> Lye listening to the never ceasing song
> That day nor night neer wearys into rest
> But hums unceasingly the summer long.[27]

Sound, sight, and motion coalesce in these lines, but motion dominates the union. The three successive stressed accents in "one broad gleam" in the description of the sky slow down the verse as they do when describing the meadows as "green rich sweeping." But once the scene moves on to the less static stream the verse is released to flow evenly to the full stop after "long." The second section of the poem is less satisfactory, declining into a jingling couplet at the end, but these opening lines demonstrate Clare's desire to relate versification to subject matter.

More often the verse is manipulated not simply to convey motion, but to chart the reader's progress through the maze of description with which Clare presents him. To transcend the monotonous regularity of conventional units within the sonnet he found it necessary to develop a pace, a movement of language which is appropriate to the mood or attitude he wished to communicate. Such a technique was especially crucial to Clare since he sought unity of impression by composing the complete sonnet in a single sentence. In "Summer Amusements" he makes use of a combination of caesurae and run-on lines to slow the verse and to avoid the naturally rhythmic sound of regular iambic pentameter:

> I love to hide me on a spot that lies
> In solitudes were footsteps find no track
> To make intrusions—there to sympithise
> With nature—often gazing on the rack
> That veils the bluness of the summer skies
> In rich varietys—or oer the grass
> Behold the spangld crowds of butterflyes
> Flutter from flower to flower—and things that pass
> In urgent travel by my still retreat
> The bustling beetle tribes—and up the stem
> Of bents see lady cows with nimble feet
> Climb tall church steeple heights or more to them
> Till at its quaking top they take their seat
> Which bows and off they flye fresh happiness to meet.[28]

Not until the ninth line do we get a substantial pause at the end
of a line, and we are given no chance to fall into a rigid pattern of
phrases and clauses. This is a poem of pace, one in which our
response to the scene is controlled by the poet's manipulation of
our progress through the poem. The disruption of regular lines
reflects the precise way in which Clare's mind reacts to his
experience. Each phrase adds a new image and each phrase,
different in its length and position in the line, attracts our
attention to a new feature of his thought. And the progression
through these phrases is commensurate with the tone of a
ruminating mind surveying the activity around him and gradually
focusing on the fascinating predominance of the ladybirds. Even
the final line, an alexandrine, by dragging out the length of the
line, supports the concept of ladybirds extending their flight
beyond this scene to another.

Among these mature sonnets of Clare's a few stand out as
consummate achievements of his individual adaptation of the
form. One of these is "Sand Martin," a poem that conveys a
single, though complex, impression of life in a wasteland, through
a careful manipulation of diction and syntax:

> Thou hermit haunter of the lonely glen
> And common wild and heath—the desolate face
> Of rude waste landscapes far away from men
> Where frequent quarrys give thee dwelling place
> With strangest taste and labour undeterred
> Drilling small holes along the quarrys side
> More like the haunts of vermin than a bird
> And seldom by the nesting boy descried
> Ive seen thee far away from all thy tribe
> Flirting about the unfrequented sky
> And felt a feeling that I cant describe
> Of lone seclusion and a hermit sky
> To see thee circle round nor go beyond
> That lone heath and its melancholly pond.[29]

There is a trace here of the octave-sestet division that Clare was
fond of earlier in his career, the former describing the
environment of the bird and the latter expressing the poet's
response to the bird and its home. But the dominant impression
belies that division, giving a unified picture of bird and landscape

as they react upon the poet's mind. This is not a bird that would catch the eye of Shelley or Keats; there is nothing transcendent about its song, nor is its habitat "some melodious plot of beechen green." Rather it is a world undesirable to others, suitable only for vermin, not even rewarding for Clare's omnipresent "nesting boys." For Clare is not interested in transcendence, only in the suitability of environment to the life it supports and in the character of a bird who finds its security and pleasure in a seemingly alien location.

The special quality that distinguishes this poem is its clear vision into the stark life of a creature that shares Clare's world. Through a brief, largely indirect, description of the bird and a more detailed picture of its environment we are introduced to its peculiar quality of life. The severity of the scene is appealing; the cacophonic description creates a harsh tone in keeping with Clare's attempt to convince us of the reality, not the beauty, of the bird's situation. He does so by weaving a texture of sound and meaning which evokes a sense of the sand martin's remote and barren, but strangely fascinating world. Most of the basic strains are concentrated initially into the first two lines, then are skillfully dispersed through repetition into the remainder of the poem. Thus the "hermit joy" that Clare confesses in line twelve echoes his description of the bird's lifestyle in the opening line. The choice of the word "haunting" to indicate the bird's activity in that same line is ominously reflected in its association with vermin in line seven. Even the concept of loneliness is repeated later in the poem and gathers evocative power by its relation to the heath, itself a term repeated late in the poem.

A more crucial, because thematically suggestive, repetition is evident in the use Clare makes of the rather unpoetic polysyllable "unfrequented." Not only does the metrical strain on the pronunciation of the word draw our attention to its significance, the fact that it reminds us of the "frequent quarries" of line four illuminates the two facets of the bird's life that appeal to Clare. The proliferation of quarries offers the bird numerous potential dwelling places—if not a sense of community life, at least the possibility of colonies of other birds. Contrasted to that life is the bird's appearance in the isolation of the "unfrequented sky," far away, as Clare points out, "from all [its] tribe." The poet responds to two interrelated characteristics of the sand martin's life: the harsh surroundings in which it chooses to live and its ability to function in isolation.

The impact of the poem, however, relies on the effect these glimpses of the bird has on the poet. His response is not a cliché-ridden empathy, but an understanding of the character of the bird's existence, a convincing reaction that emanates out of the descriptive terminology he uses. The subtle character of Clare's response is concisely expressed as "hermit joy." A hermit's pleasure is presumably not frenetic but a quiet contentment resulting from his elimination of the tribulations of the social world and his satisfaction at having found at last his appropriate place on earth. Thus Clare's joy comes with his insight into the sand martin's satisfaction with the limits of his life, with his apparently voluntary restriction to the region of pond and heath. The hermit, unlike the outcast, chooses his situation. It is important to note, therefore, that only the heath, the pond, and the glen are lonely and melancholy; no such attributes are given to the bird. On the contrary, he is pictured as a content inhabitant of that landscape and his serenity is what impresses the poet. Thus Clare links the hermit joy with a feeling of "lone seclusion"—not loneliness, but a desirable solitude away from the haunts of men.

The pace of the poem is beautifully controlled, not by Clare's punctuation—he did not punctuate the manuscript—but by his choice of words which manipulates our ability to move through the poem. His emphasis on the first syllable of "haunter," for example, is reinforced by the natural pause that follows the introductory salutation to the bird. The syllable is drawn out, slowing down the verse while it establishes in our minds the predominant haunting quality of the poem, before it sweeps over the subsequent monosyllables leading to the shorter, but still lengthy, initial vowel of "lonely." Likewise the second line enforces our perception of the scene's desolation by injecting the adjective "wild" after, rather than before, the noun it modifies. That placement of the long "i," coupled with the division of the series of "glen," "common," and "heath" by the repetition of "and," accentuates the length of the adjective. Thereafter the momentum of the verse accelerates from the poem's only visually marked pause, the dash in line two, but only until the succession of three heavily stressed syllables in "rude, waste landscapes" once more arrests our ear. The subsequent succession of phrases falls into place regularly if not smoothly until the full stop after "described."

But these phrases are not syntactically united into a coherent sentence. The fifth and sixth lines obviously refer to the bird, whereas the other lines describe the landscape. This may cause initial confusion in reading, but the effect is not entirely disconcerting; the impression remains unified with the three elements of the description interrelating with each other. The final six lines, no longer intended to be so evocatively descriptive, convey Clare's response in regular phrases logically and syntactically linked. They comprise a series of statements that follow each other almost inevitably, each revealing a new dimension of Clare's insight. The metrical texture of the sestet also impresses by the easy, yet firm insistence on the placing of caesurae. In line ten the pronunciation of "unfrequented" forces a pause after the first syllable, line twelve is divided by a conjunction, line thirteen by a very effective and natural qualifying phrase, and line fourteen by another conjunction. The poem ends with an echo of the polysyllabic movement earlier felt in "unfrequented." A succession of three spondees, an anapest, and two iambs provide the appropriate conclusion by following the deliberate pace of the opening three words of the line with a local rhythm rising to the first syllable of "melancholy" and dropping off to end firmly with the strong monosyllable "pond."

In this poem the movement of the verse does not indicate a virtuoso manipulating the verse to illustrate motion which is itself the subject of the poem; rather, it demonstrates how careful Clare was to manipulate the pace at which he wanted a poem dealing with other subjects to be read. In this regard the conclusion of "Sand Martin" is particularly illuminating. The poem's principal statement appears to be complete with line twelve—Clare has finished expressing his emotional involvement with the scene—but the precise characteristic of the bird which produces that response, the final dimension of Clare's experience, is saved for the end. An impression of the bird's restraint lingers with Clare after he has formulated as much as he can of his instinctive feeling for the bird. The poem is, therefore, a progressive revelation of Clare's state of mind, much more than just a static description of a bird in a landscape.

Other sonnets of this period are equally successful at such revelation. Indeed, "Wood-Pictures in Spring," although quite different in style from "Sand Martin," is another example of Clare's unique accomplishment in the sonnet form:

> The rich brown umber hue the oaks unfold
> When springs young sunshine bathes their trunks in gold
> So rich so beautiful so past the power
> Of words to paint—my heart aches for the dower
> The pencil gives to soften and infuse
> This brown luxuriance of unfolding hues
> This living lusious tinting woodlands give
> Into a landscape that might breath and live
> And this old gate that claps against the tree
> The entrance of springs paradise should be
> Yet paint itself with living nature fails
> —The sunshine threading through these broken rails
> In mellow shades—no pencil eer conveys
> And mind alone feels fancies and pourtrays.[30]

There is a convincing fusion of subject and style in this poem. The deep, rich vowel tones in "umber," "unfold," "hues," and "infuse" convey, through sound, the depth of color he finds in this peculiar combination of oak-brown and the transforming gold of the sun's rays. The sounds we normally employ to suggest depth of vocal tone are here used to impart depth of color tone. Clare seeks a further accuracy of color by adding a softness to his evocation of browns through sibilants in "this brown luxuriance of unfolding hues / This living lusious tinting woodlands give."

The movement of the verse also contributes to the fusion of subject and expression. Although written in couplets, as an increasing number of Clare's later sonnets were, this poem lacks none of the finer qualities of pace and rhythm found in those with a more complex rhyme scheme. The succession of run-on lines and the natural, unobtrusive rhymes assure an easy, fluid reading characteristic of only the masters of the couplet. After a general statement of facts in the opening two lines, the verse seizes on the beauty of the scene and moves urgently through the next eight lines, gathering special impetus in lines seven and eight. This movement reflects the eagerness of the poet to capture and infuse—to meld—all elements of the scene into an individual impression. At the same time he is struggling with the apparent inadequacy of his medium. He lacks the color of paint or the shading facility of the pencil to render his momentary perception into a static representation of what he sees. Poetry has the disadvantage of requiring time to convey the scene, hence his attempt to move as quickly as possible through the verse and to force as much as possible of the description into a single sentence.

The poem is, therefore, a partial contradiction of what Clare feels is the weakness of this type of art. In spite of his misgivings, the poem does communicate the uniqueness of the scene, not only the blending of color but also the sense of development in time which transcends the static picture of the painter or sketcher. Thus the color, revealing itself gradually in time, "unfolds," just as the details of the specific scene reveal themselves gradually. Barrell's complaint that the image of the clapping gate "[seems] strangely separate from the rest of the poem and the images around [it]"[31] is therefore unjustified. The image, whether it is picturesque as he charges or not, fits into the unfolding description which coexists with the thematic statement of the poem. We are presented with the oak trees first, then with Clare's reaction to their beauty, with the gate and its motion—another detail impossible to convey with paint or pencil—and finally with the effect of sunshine on what we are now told are "broken" rails of the gate. Clare has focused on the active element in the scene, both the color unfolding with the progress of spring and the landscape unfolding to the sight of the observer. He has demonstrated, ironically, the facility that his art possesses in excess of the visual artist's, to communicate his unique response to nature.

The final effect of fusion in this poem comes in the last line. The mind alone, Clare asserts, forms the center of all elements perceived, it fuses the motion with the static moment and the variety of immediately perceptible colors into an experience of "unfolding" color. And the mind does so in progressive stages, reacting emotionally ("feels"), perceiving through the imagination ("fancies"), and expressing artistically ("pourtrays"). The poem is a celebration of the imaginative powers of the mind; both in the complexity and content of its theme and in the quality of its versification, it deserves consideration with the best sonnets of the major Romantics.

The faint suggestion, in the concluding lines of "Wood-Pictures in Spring," that Clare is referring to the effect on him of the poetic process is clarified by other, more obvious, references in sonnets of the same period. He seems to have considered the sonnet a convenient vehicle for expressing his faith in the transforming power of that process. Thus his natural descriptions frequently conclude with statements, often mystical in their overtones, about the effect his response to the scene has had on his mind. This tendency explains the final tercet of "Salters Tree." That poem describes an elm tree with "rifted trunk all notched and scarred" and dwells on its ability to lift Clare out of his present worries by reminding him of past happiness near the tree. The theme is not a novel one for Clare, but it concludes with an impressive visionary image:

> The wind in that eternal ditty sings
> Humming of future things that burns the mind
> To leave some fragment of itself behind.[32]

From natural description and personal reflection he turns to an expression of the ecstasy of poetic composition. In particular, he focuses on that point in the process where, as he outlines elsewhere, genius inspires "a pleasing rapture of the mind / A kindling warmth to learning unconfin'd."[33] In "Salters Tree" his reference to the poetic process unites Clare's imaginative response to the tree with his personal desire to recapture the past. In other of the sonnets similar references are less satisfactorily integrated with the theme of the poem. In "The Morning Wind," for instance, he fails to specify what he means by "feeling's fairy visions" or to relate them clearly to the poem's subject.[34] And in several other sonnets fleeting, but suggestive phrases imply a profundity of insight into the mental activity that produces his art—an insight that is belied by the rest of the poem.

Accompanying his concern with the elusive subject of the poetic process was an increasing propensity to add a dimension of mysticism to his landscape descriptions. That Blakean quality so often noticed in his asylum lyrics occurs in brief touches in these earlier sonnets. Such a visionary tendency reveals itself in

"The Instinct of Hope" where he deduces from natural phenomena a spiritual certainty of orthodox Christianity.[35] In "Pleasant Places," too, a single suggestive phrase elevates Clare's normal observations to a visionary level:

> While painting winds to make compleat the scene
> In rich confusion mingles every green
> Waving the sketchy pencil in their hands
> Shading the living scenes to fairy lands.[36]

His catalogue of picturesque images, not quoted here, is broken off by his observation of the wind transforming the immediate scene into a bewitching "fairy" landscape. Perhaps the essence of such mysticism is just that inability to explain, but Clare's later lyrics, like most of Blake's songs, manage to indicate more precisely the essential direction of their mystical vision. Clare had not yet developed this ability to render his insights in explicit enough terms.

The contrast between the earlier descriptive sonnets and those written in the asylum is immediately obvious in "Sonnet: I Am." We cannot be sure whether Clare intended these lines to form a continuation of the three stanzas entitled "I Am," or to stand separately, perhaps as a companion poem. In the Knight Transcripts, far from following "straight on from *I Am* without a break," as Tibble states in a footnote to his edition of the poems, it appears on a separate page.[37] In a later copy made from Knight's notebooks it follows directly, but that version is one step further removed from the original. Furthermore, Clare seems to have titled these lines "Sonnet: I Am" to distinguish them from the other poem which is not a sonnet, unless Knight took upon himself the responsibility of naming them. Even in that case he must have considered that Clare intended a separate sonnet if the term in his title means anything at all. Certainly the tone of the sonnet is distinct from that of the other poem; the confidence in personal existence which Clare finds reassuring in the longer poem is replaced in the sonnet by a questioning uncertainty in the opening four lines. And that hesitancy is sufficient to undermine what confidence he does claim in lines six and fourteen.

Besides this tone, however, the subject itself is characteristic of the later sonnets. The concrete descriptions of earlier sonnets are replaced by a nightmarish, visionary view of a detached body wandering through "Earth's prison" and suffering from a potion of "dullness":

> I feel I am, I only know I am
> And plod upon the earth as dull and void
> Earth's prison chilled my body with its dram
> Of dullness, and my soaring thoughts destroyed.
> I fled to solitudes from passions dream
> But strife persued—I only know I am.[38]

The traumatic picture of Clare's predicament terminates abruptly here with his reassertion of faith in his own identity. With the repetition of "I only know I am" he gains the confidence to describe, albeit with mystical vagueness, his place in the universe:

> I was a being created in the race
> Of men disdaining bounds of place and time—
> A spirit that could travel o'er the space
> Of earth and heaven—like a thought sublime,
> Tracing creation, like my maker, free—
> A soul unshackled like eternity,
> Spurning earth's vain and soul debasing thrall
> But now I only know I am—that's all.

The final line reiterates the theme of which he finds it so necessary to convince himself. And his parting shot, "that's all," gains emphasis not only from the colloquial form of its expression, but also from the force of understatement. The "all" that separates his former from his present position is an awesome gulf indeed.

A similar autobiographical introspection and cosmic imagery form the basis of another sonnet from the asylum, "Written in Prison." "Inured to strife and hardships from a child," he writes in that poem, "I traced with lonely steps the desert wild."[39] A more jocular view of his situation, a new variation from his traditional sonnet tone, emerges from "To John Clare." He begins with a hearty question, "Well, honest John, how fare you now at home," and answers it with a catalogue description of scenes and details which he has enjoyed when younger and living at home.[40] Beyond these few sonnets, however, the asylum years have little to yield in fourteen-line poems; the great form of that period was the lyric.

To appreciate fully his achievement in the sonnet we must remember the sonnets of an earlier part of his career. They place his innovations at the culminating point of a long history of change in the sonnet. Wordsworth, recognizing Milton's departure from the Italian influence, also indicates his own individual development of the form in a letter to Alexander Dyce, the editor of *Specimens of English Sonnets* (1833):

In the better half of his sonnets the sense does not close with the rhyme at the eighth line, but overflows into the second portion of the metre. Now it has struck me, that this is not done merely to gratify the ear by variety and freedom of sound, but also to aid in giving that pervading sense of intense Unity in which the excellence of the Sonnet has always seemed to me mainly to consist. Instead of looking at this composition as a piece of architecture, making a whole out of three parts, I have been much in the habit of preferring the image of an orbicular body,—a sphere—or a dew-drop.[41]

As we have seen, Clare pushed this quality of the sonnet to its limit, creating poems of a single movement capturing an evocative scene at a precise moment of perception, while at the same time conveying the transient sense of motion contained in that instant. His work belongs with the other major nineteenth-century innovators of the sonnet, Wordsworth before him and Gerard Manley Hopkins after.

CHAPTER 5

Growing into Song

I *Two Traditions*

THE predominant lyrical note in Clare's best poetry grew out of the musical atmosphere that pervaded the village culture of his youth. Frequently in his later period of mature creativity, he was to acknowledge the influence of music on his composition of songs such as "Peggy Band." He refused to alter his version of that piece because it had been composed "in memory of the music."[1] What applied to individual songs like "Peggy Band" also governed his inspiration to write poetry in general:

The spirit of fame of living a little after life like a name on a conspicuous place urges my blood upward into unconscious melodys & striding down my orchard & homestead I hum & sing inwardly those little madrigals & then go in & pen them down thinking them much better things than they are until I look over them again & then the charm vanishes into the vanity that I shall do somthing better ere I die & so in spite of myself I rhyme on & write nothing but little things at last.[2]

The context of this passage seems to deny Storey's implication that the "little things" are sonnets.[3] Obviously what Clare finds diminutive about the verse composed in this manner is its quality, not its length. Furthermore, his other comments linking musical activity with the poetic process refer only to lyrics and songs, the types of poetry for which he found his musical background most valuable. Occasionally this musical contribution was made by mundane rhythmical sounds like those that influenced his writing of "Swamps of Wild Rushes": "I measured this ballad to-day wi the thrumming of my mothers wheel if it be tinctured wi the drone of that domestic music you will excuse it after this confession."[4] More often the lyrics stem from his saturation in

122

two musical traditions which encouraged the naturally retiring young Clare to participate in the cultural life around him.

Throughout Clare's autobiographical writings we catch glimpses of the young farm laborer walking, fiddle under his arm, to or from village dances; or we find him trekking to Drury's shop at Stamford to get new tunes to practice. He developed this interest naturally; his ancestors were "gardeners parish clerks & fiddlers."[5] Clare himself played at local dances, even, he records, getting his second sight of Patty, his future wife, while walking to a Stamford dance. The fiddle was also his motivation for a lengthy friendship with the groups of gypsies who frequented the Helpston neighborhood: "I usd to spend my Sundays & summer evenings among them learning to play the fiddle in their manner by the ear & fancy."[6] James Hessey, one of Clare's publishers, recognized Clare's dedication to this type of music by giving him a new violin, possibly made by one of the renowned craftsmen of Cremona, in April, 1820. His previous fiddle remained "like an old friend" reminding him of "what is past many pains and pleasures mingled together in banished days."[7] By the end of 1820 he was congratulating himself on his competence with the new instrument:

I get on 'like a house afire' with my 'Cremoni' & begin to be stil'd a first rate scraper among my rustic companions tho in fact I dont play one tune in 20 by notes she makes a rare noise & thats plenty—a professional at Stamford tells me she's a valuable instrument & her equal is not easy to be met with in our parts so when I go into quarrelsome company I take my own scraper for fear the other shoud be broken.[8]

His proficiency with dance music was not forgotten when composing his poetry. The contact with gypsies provided him with music to popular songs—"got the tune of 'Highland Mary' from Wisdom Smith a gipsey & pricked another sweet tune without name as he fiddled it"[9]—which in turn influenced the rhythms of his literary verse: "I have got in this dancing measure which runs so easy that I can hardly get out of it several of my summer walks & 'Helpstone Heath' which I am now [Feb., 1823] writing are in the same."[10] The true extent of this influence is difficult to ascertain; the excessive rhythmicality which mars several of his poems probably results from his propensity to "hear" the tune as he wrote, but the more subtle measures, by their very subtlety, are difficult to trace through Clare's modification to their source in such a boldly rhythmic style of music.

Clare's debt to the oral tradition is more easily traced and more central to an understanding of his lyrics. Few poets have experienced the oral literature of semiliterate rural England as genuinely as Clare did. His parents were both singers of ballads, his father's repertoire being especially large, and he spent much of his working time in the fields listening to old women singing traditional songs as they worked. He also observed the impact of oral poetry on the emotional lives of his fellow villagers: "these very people will stand around an old ballad singer & with all the romantic enthusiasm of pity shed tears over the doggerel tales of imaginary distress."[11] Forming part of the crowd himself on occasion, the young poet gained an appreciation of the relationship between music and poetry which controlled much of the lyricism in his own work. His comments on "Peggy Band" reveal just how deep his understanding of this relationship was:

The old song alluded to is 'Peggy *Band*' there is a song of modern date thats call'd 'Peggy Bond' but tis nothing like the old one neither in words or music for the tune of the old one is Capital as my father used to sing it but I cannot say much for the words for you know the best of our old English ballads thats preserved by the memorys of our rustics (whatever they might have been) are so mutilated that they scarcly rise to mediocrity while their melodys are beautiful & the more I hear them the more I wish Id skill enough in music to prick them down.[12]

Although this passage undervalues the verbal impact of many traditional ballads, Clare is aware of the relative inadequacy of unlettered musicians to preserve the poetic quality of their words. At the same time he appreciates the enduring beauty of their melodies. What is more revealing in this passage, however, is his conviction that both music and words are essential criteria for judging the comparative worth of the two songs. In his own writing he demonstrated his appreciation of the music by filling two notebooks with transcriptions of traditional melodies, and of the words by devoting his career to the writing of lyrics.

His first poems were "imitations of [his] father's songs"[13] and from that beginning the oral tradition continued to influence his development as a poet. He found it necessary, even, to introduce his early poetry to his parents under the guise of an "imitation of some popular song" in order to get their honest opinion of its value.[14] Gradually, however, he incorporated his own material into the traditional forms, dispensing with the conventions in favor of expressing personal emotions: "as my feelings grew into song I felt a desire to preserve them."[15] Growing into song is the story of his career; it was no accident that the form of his mature period was predominantly the lyric.

II *Ballads*

A gift of Percy's *Reliques,* from the Stamford bookseller Edward Drury, in the summer of 1820, confirmed Clare's interest in the old ballads and songs. "The tales [were] familiar from childhood," he told Hessey, and "all the stories of my grandmother & her gossiping neighbours I find versified in these vols."[16] Four years later he was still reading the poems and ballads in Percy, but more critically now and with more awareness of their affinity with his own aspirations after clarity of emotional expression: I "take them up as often as I may I am always delighted there is so much of the essence & simplicity of true poetry that makes me regret I did not see them sooner as they would have formed my taste & laid the foundations of my judgment in writing and thinking poetically as it is I feel indebted to them for many feelings."[17] Clare had written his own ballads before this date, but none as accomplished as those that followed. Some of these later poems are worth looking at closely as examples of Clare's delicate lyrical touch in poems that impress by their narrative economy and metrical simplicity.

Most of them, like many traditional ballads, are laments over lost or unrequited love, expressions of passion tinged with regret or sorrow. In one of these laments we can see something of Clare's artistry in fusing ballad techniques with his own imaginative sense of form:

> 'Twas somewhere in the April time
>   Not long before the May
> A sitting on a bank o' thyme
>   I heard a maiden say

My truelove is a sailor
    And e're he went away
We spent a year together
    And here my lover lay—

The gold furze were in blossom
    So was the daisey too
The dew pearls on the little flowers
    Were emeralds in hue
On this same summer morning
    Though then the sabath day
He cropt me spring polanthuses
    Beneath the white thorn may

He cropt me spring polanthuses
    And said if they would keep
They'd tell me all loves fusses
    For dews on them did weep
And I did weep at parting
    Which lasted all the week
And when he turned for starting
    My full heart could not speak

The same roots grow polanthus flowers
    Beneath the same haw tree
I cropt them in morns dewy hours
    And here loves offerings be
Oh come to me my sailor beau
    And ease my aching breast
The storms shall cease to rave and blow
    And here thy life find rest.[18]

The dramatic framework established in the first four lines, while perhaps more typical of Romantic literary ballads, is not unknown to traditional balladry. It immediately sets before us the significance of time in the poem, not only the time of the year, but the length of the earlier love affair and the relationship between the present lament and the original plighting of love exactly a year earlier. The abrupt leaps in time (between the first and second and then the third and fourth stanzas), themselves characteristic of the leaping and lingering techniques of the ballad, are conveyed economically by means of simple tense shifts. Thus the change to "were" in stanza two is the sole indicator that we are being taken back in time, and the reversal in stanza four indicates a similarly abrupt return to the present. A further economy is evident in the girl's use of the present tense when identifying her lover's occupation—that she says he "is" a sailor reveals her faith in his eventual return. The temporal preoccupation of the poem does not end there. Clare's theme hinges on our interpretation of the sailor's prophecy. The inability of cropped polyanthuses to withstand time, the girl's faith in the regeneration of planted flowers, and the sailor's pledge depending on the cut variety, all lead to the conclusion that she has been misled. She has misunderstood the hidden implications of the talisman, has been duped like many another ballad heroine. On the other hand, she manifests that her love has withstood a year's absence from her lover.

In this relationship Clare has carefully interwoven the relativity of time with his narrative technique. Between the two leaps in time, already mentioned, are two stanzas of very effective "lingering" over the emotional character of the original experience. This effect is achieved by the repetition of complete lines (lines 15 and 17) and of individual words ("weep" in lines 20 and 21), as well as the use of "filler" lines (repeating the sense of a line without adding new information, as in line 10).

This narrative method and its relation to the subject of time parallel a gradual development of the emotion being expressed. Clare seems to have understood what M. J. C. Hodgart calls the "counterpoint of ballads," in which "the story moves forward in bounds, against a background of regular stanzaic melody and against the formal patterning of folk art."[19] Usually the stanzaic melody depends on the haunting tunes of musical ballads to slow down and control the movement through stanzas which otherwise read rather quickly. Writing poetry rather than song, Clare achieved a similar control without the aid of an accompanying tune. The disclosure of emotion in this ballad is structurally delayed; with each paired stanza the intensity of emotion increases, parallel to, but independent from the narrative. The essence of the story is contained in the first stanza, but the sorrow revealed there is only that which derives from the general situation of a departed lover. The second eight lines add the girl's association of love with nature, the sabbath, and especially the polyanthus which has been dear to her and the sailor. Not until the third stanza, however, do we learn the depth of her attachment to that flower and the dependence of her future on the interpretation of the ambivalent prophecy connected with it. Finally, in the last stanza the girl's statement of faith, undercut by the irony of her lover's prophecy, is acted out as she picks the flowers again. The depths of her grief, to which her lament has been gradually descending since the opening stanza, are evoked in the concluding suggestion that her love is sufficient to overcome storms and distance, which she presumes have kept them apart.

No such hope breaks through the sensitive, understated lament in another of Clare's best ballads, entitled simply "Ballad." A young girl's casual encounter with a deceiving lover has left her a wiser, yet melancholy, woman:

> I dreamt not what it was to woo
> And felt my heart secure
> Till Robin dropt a word or two
> Last evening on the moor
> Though with no flattering words the while
> His suit he urged to move
> Fond ways informed me with a smile
> How sweet it was to love
>
> He left the path to let me pass
> The dropping dews to shun
> And walked himself among the grass
> I deemed it kindly done
> And when his hand was held to me
> As oer each stile we went
> I deemed it rude to say him nay
> And manners to consent
>
> He saw me to the town and then
> He sighed but kissed me not
> And whispered 'we shall meet agen'
> But did'n't say for what
> Yet on my breast his cheek had lain
> And though it gently prest
> It bruised my heart and left a pain
> That robs it of its rest.[20]

The obvious ballad characteristics which Clare draws upon, the approximation of a ballad stanza here coupled into eight-line units, the narrative leap between stanzas two and three with its enormous suggestive power of something sexual occurring which the girl's modesty forbids her narrating, the sense of personal injury emanating from the song's being sung the day after the encounter, and the consistently understated descriptions of their actions are bound together into a tight structure by the subtle, though convincing, disclosure of the personality of the two lovers.

The girl's character is traditional. She is one of a long line of victims in the ballads, victims like Lizzy Wan, Bonnie Annie, Lord Randall's daughter, or the Fair Flower of Northumberland. But she has a living personality, too, one that is dramatized through her self-revelatory monologue. We are given an indication of her weaknesses, especially the tragic naïveté which precipitates her present state of mind. She has been inexperienced ("I dreamt not what it was to woo") and overly deferential (she concedes her virtue to avoid rudeness), susceptible not to the obvious flattery of words, but to the kind gesture and the winning smile. This naïveté in the first two thirds of the poem makes the wound expressed in the final stanza especially poignant. We begin to see the callous, designing nature of Robin's actions; the smile and the assisting hand are revealed for what they are by his neglect to kiss her as they part and by her suspicions about his motives for wanting to meet her again. The final image of the bruised heart is at once an effective conclusion to the ballad and an embodiment of the nature of their passion. Even their passion is typical of the ballad tradition, evoking the violence of emotion beneath the tranquil appearance of love.

Both these ballads reveal stark passions with a subtlety and economy which enhance the impact of that emotion. The poignancy coupled with irony that characterizes the best ballads, "The Unquiet Grave" or "Lord Randall," is captured in these. They contain little of the awkward or redundant phrase or the clumsy moralizing of some of Clare's other verse. Hodgart has pointed out the pathos of the folk tradition which "shows a complete lack of protest or of sentimentality," and he argues that the "technical components [of the ballad] are really effective only in their context; and that context is a special cultural and artistic tradition."[21] Clare lived in that tradition. He had the scholar's interest in ballad collecting, but his peasant way of life also helped him assimilate the pathos inherent in that cultural tradition. Hodgart never mentions Clare, but he is describing Clare's best ballads when he writes in general that "the height of the ballad art is reached when [the] imaginative beauty of folk-tradition is caught and fixed by skilled poets, poets able to keep the essentials of tradition and unite them with the literary graces."[22]

III Songs

The bulk of Clare's other nondescriptive verse falls into two groups, the conventional love songs which he seems to have written as readily to casual acquaintances as to the real passion of his life, and the distinctly individual lyrics which examine the range and depth of his personal emotional experience. Poems in the former group are often overlooked because they are too conventional, or too similar to each other in subject matter and treatment, or simply because they are not subtle lyrics like those in the second, quite different, group. But Cecil Day Lewis, in his lucid and discriminating analysis of the distinction between songs and lyrical poems, argues for the virtues of simplicity and purity in poems which rely on musical cadences, argues for the legitimacy of what he calls the "lyric impulse." To him the lyric (what I will call "song" to differentiate it from the more sophisticated form which he calls "lyrical poem") is a "poem written for music . . . or simply with music at the back of the poet's mind."[23] Clare's admissions, quoted earlier in this chapter, about the role of music in his poetic composition confirm his qualifications for writing such poetry, even without our assessment of the other features of Day Lewis's definition. These features include a lack of complexity in syntax, an absence of irony or other "cerebral matter," and an impersonality that reveals itself in a "stylised" expression of the poet's emotion. In short, the "saying of only one thing at a time, without reservations, modifying parentheses, mental complications of any kind, is the lyric's chief term of reference."[24] By these standards Clare's best songs are rare songs indeed.

We have seen that Clare was a semiprofessional fiddler; he also tried his hand at professional song writing. Drury first suggested that Clare write songs and arranged for a contemporary composer, J. Power, to set the resulting words to music. Clare variously mentions his motivation for complying with

Drury's request as "a matter of course for a livelihood," or his
thinking it "a fine thing to have one's name on a music sheet," or
as a form of "recompence for the suppos'd injury done [Drury]
in forcing" the original copyright of his poems out of Drury's
hands.[25] Whatever his true motivation, he approached the
project with his usual alternation of feverish creativity and
debilitating ennui. He wrote to Hessey in July, 1820, that he
aimed at composing one hundred of these songs (he called them
ballads with his usual indiscriminate use of the term) and was
writing six or eight a day, having already completed seventy.[26] At
other times he wrote to Taylor asking for advice "either to stop
me or to set me off at full gallop," or to Hessey that "I intend to
try at songs again when the fit comes on me but God knows when
that will be, I don't."[27] At least one of his songs was set to music
by Haydn Corri and sung at Covent Garden by Madame Vestris.
Another, "The Banks of Broomsgrove," was set to music by a
composer named Barnett and published by Power.[28] But by and
large Clare was not happy with Power's corruption of the songs
he wrote for Drury: "a Mutilated Skeleton of one of the Songs
which made me so d—d mad that I am half sorry I wrote my
answer at the moment—Still if I see my merit at stake I am aright
to cry stop thief—I stopt him however . . . I said if his music man
lik'd to take the words as he found em they was there—if not let
them alone for my Name should never accompany such
affectation & conciet."[29] He even went so far as to ask Taylor to
publish some of the songs in *The Village Minstrel and Other
Poems* in order to have the correct version of them on record.[30]

The major consequence of these hours of composition was yet
another heartache for Clare. Although the publishers, Welch
and Hames, claim to have paid Drury for the songs, he seems
never to have passed the payment along. A financial wrangle
ensued, involving Clare, Taylor, Hessey, and Drury, the only
result of which was Clare's disillusionment: "I wish [the songs]
had never been published at all for they brought me neither
credit nor profit."[31] By January of 1824 he was energetically
planning several projects, among them the one hundred sonnets,
but he conspicuously omits any references to song writing.[32]
However little it contributed to his financial position or his
public reputation, though, the practice of writing such a large
number of songs in a relatively short period of time honed his
talent for concise expression of emotion, and produced several

superb songs noted for the purity and clarity of their diction and the metrical simplicity of their lyric style.

These qualities are evident in a song like "Meet me in the Green Glen," where the poet's emotion is at once personal and conventional. We feel the urgency of the passion which has inspired his outburst, but at the same time we see his cry in the context of lovers throughout the love-song tradition. We are given no picture of the human object of his love, no reasons for his love, no declaration of constancy, no information extraneous to his immediate need to see her again:

> Love meet me in the green glen
> > Beside the tall Elm tree
> Where the Sweet briar smells so sweet agen
> > There come wi me
> > > Meet me in the green glen
>
> Meet me at the sunset
> > Down in the green glen
> Where we've often met
> > By hawthorn tree and foxes den
> > > Meet me in the green glen
>
> Meet me by the sheep pen
> > Where briars smell at een
> Meet me i the green glen
> > Where white thorn shades are green
> > > Meet me in the green glen
>
> Meet me in the green glen
> > By sweet briar bushes there
> Meet me by your own sen
> > Where the wild thyme blossoms fair
> > > Meet me in the green glen
>
> Meet me by the sweet briar
> > By the mole hill swelling there
> When the west glows like a fire
> > Gods crimson bed is there
> > > Meet me in the green glen.[33]

The purity of expression here leaves little for commentary. The tone is plaintive; not altogether confident of the woman's response to his urgency, the speaker is at the same time filled with tenderness and nostalgia for their previous meetings. The force of his passion reaches us through the repetition both of the title line and of the references to the sweetbrier, but is controlled by the precision of time and place that the speaker insists upon. Their meeting must be precisely right. It must occur beside a specific patch of sweetbrier in their familiar glen, at the precise time of sunset and in the season in which the sweetbrier blossoms. This particularity moderates the passion, imposing a sense of order on the emotion the speaker so strongly feels. The force of his passion accumulates through the poem, too, gathering urgency with each repetition of the refrain until we are left at the end with the anxiously imperative "Meet me in the green glen." The falling rhythm of this ending suggests, by its weakness, the quiet weariness of the speaker after his repeated plea.

The theme of "Meet me in the Green Glen" is characteristic of Clare's songs. Taken together, they explore the subject of love in all its complexity. Some treat love in the context of a clearly defined situation, as this one does; others examine it with a theme in mind, attempting to communicate what Clare has learned through his own experiences with women. "Love Lives Beyond the Tomb," for example, exudes confidence in the permanence of personal love-relationships, whereas others, like "The Poet's Love," convey the anguish and uncertainty Clare often felt when involved with women:

> What is Love but pains disguise
> That dares not tell its secret pain
> That ever shrinks from hearts replies
> And tries to be himself again
> That shuns the crowd and noises rude
> That tries to keep his thoughts unknown
> And in the green of Solitude
> Keeps loves dear bondage all his own
>
> There is but one in all the world
> Search earth or ocean clouds or air
> With rosey cheek and ringlets curled
> That seems to him so passing fair
> Grace in her motion—music speaks
> When e'er she talks or binds her hair
> The fairest rose blooms on her cheeks
> Her breasts the whitest lilies wear

> The Poet is a silent thing
> A man in love none knoweth where
> He sees her in the boiling spring
> At even on the blooming brere
> He hears her in the songs of birds
> He sees her in the evening sky
> A shepherdess among the herds
> A milkmaid wi' the grazing kye.[34]

Again the emotion, while it evokes a sense of real personal anguish, is contained in a rather conventional statement about the supremacy of ideal womanhood. That "she" is conventional rather than a specific woman is clear from the vague description which, though it concentrates on her physical beauty, gives no personal details, preferring general comments on her graceful motion and musical voice. The very conventionality of these epithetical descriptions ("rosy cheek," "ringlets curled," and lily-white breasts) is the point of the poem. The ideal woman is a type, a muse, the source of a poet's, as opposed to an ordinary man's, love. She transcends the merely physical and individual. She is what enables him to overcome the pain he describes in the first stanza even though she is also the source of the pain, at once his inspiration and his bane.

In Clare's scheme of things this muse is often given substantial form, although the poetic woman usually bears little resemblance to the real person on whom she is based. The most constant theme addressed to these women is that of his personal devotion to one of them. In "The Secret," for instance, he celebrates the impact of a nameless woman on his vision of beauty. The first two stanzas, written in the past tense, describe his propensity to use his lover's identity as a measure of beauty in other women:

> I loved thee tho I told thee not
> Right earlily and long
> Thou wert my joy in every spot
> My theme in every song
>
> And when I saw a stranger face
> Where beauty held the claim
> I gave it like a secret grace
> The being of thy name.[35]

For Clare his lover is synonymous with beauty, therefore he imposes her identity on every beautiful face he sees.

By shifting from the past to the present tense Clare indicates a lapse of time between these two stanzas and the third. At present the singer has reversed the habit described in the preceding stanzas. He now uses other beautiful women to help his memory recall his original love:

> And all the charms of face or voice
> Which I in others see
> Are but the reccolected choice
> Of what I felt for thee.

In addition, the sight of a beautiful face now reminds him not of the physical beauty of his lover's face, but of the original emotion he felt for her. The passing of time has altered the effect of his love; the secret of his passion has forced him to seek external, physical reminders of his past love which continue to stimulate his vicarious emotional life.

In other poems Clare identifies Mary Joyce as the chief inspiration of his love songs. Although he vowed in a letter to Dr. Matthew Allen that "almost every song I write has some sighs or wishes in ink about Mary,"[36] he directed his theme of devotion toward other women as well, often to casual acquaintances who only added their name to a poem about love in general. But he also wrote a few songs of personal devotion to his wife, Patty. In the following example a hymn-like measure in the back of Clare's mind contributes to the solemn tone of his sentiment:

> Maid of Walkherd, meet agen,
> By the wilding in the glen,
> By the oak against the door,
> Where we often met before;
> By the bosom's heaving snow,
> By thy fondness none shall know,
> Maid of Walkherd, meet agen
> By the wilding in the glen.
>
> By thy hand of slender make,
> By thy love I'll ne'er forsake,
> By thy heart I'll ne'er betray,
> Let me kiss thy fears away!

> I will live and love thee ever,
> Leave thee and forsake thee never;
> Though far in other lands to be,
> Yet never far from love and thee.[37]

The phraseology and diction are faultless, attracting no undue attention to themselves, but creating through the formal "thee" and "thy" a poem of dedication. The sureness of Clare's touch is enhanced by the repetition. It not only serves the solemnity of the poem, but also adds its own subtleties. Thus the repetition of "by" at the beginning of several lines indicates the shifting emphasis of Clare's thought. At first the word only delineates the location of the anticipated meeting, but with lines five and six we begin to sense an additional meaning. It still describes a place—he wishes to be beside her physically—but it also serves as a pledge—by her bosom, fondness, love, etc., he asks her to plight her love by meeting him, and he by these same tokens plights his with a kiss. The solemn tone, conveyed by meter and syntax, is what impresses us with the authenticity of Clare's feeling toward Patty. We do not need additional knowledge of the sincere feeling toward her that emerges from his letters. After their marriage, itself enforced by Patty's pregnancy, Clare's letters continually refer to his growing affection for her as a wife and companion. This poem is a personal tribute to her and, at the same time, an effective general love song which never mentions her name.

Clare's insistence on the character of the locale for their meeting in this poem is typical of his technique. His declarations of love for women are seldom divorced from their shared love of nature. In most of his songs nature is a touchstone for the quality of his love for any specific woman. Even in his simplest verse a sparse reference to natural objects frequently legitimizes his invocation of a woman's love. Objects briefly mentioned, like the sweetbrier, elm, and hawthorn trees in "Meet me in the Green Glen," or the wilding and oak in "Maid of Walkherd," are important not only because they recall the location of the lovers' previous meetings, but also because the pleasure they give is commensurate with the poet's anticipated joy in the presence of his lover. If any theme dominates the complete body of Clare's songs it is his longing for a union between himself, his lover, and nature. Nature would be enhanced by such a fusion:

> And I love all other things
> Her bright eyes look upon
> If she looks upon the hedge, or up the leafing tree
> That white thorn and the brown oak are the dearest
>   things to me.[38]

Elsewhere the poignancy of his rejection by another woman gains its effect from the disruption of this unity:

> I see thee silent talk to flowers
> The birds will sing to thee
> And lonely in these lonely hours
> You never talk to me.[39]

The absence of her love for him is measured by the tenderness of her attitude to nature. We feel through the inversion something of the depth of his sense of loss which would be more cumbersome if left to mere verbal lamentation.

When he accepted the requirements of song, its conciseness, emotional simplicity, and clarity of expression, Clare produced subtle inflections of tone from one song to another which convey the variety of his personal responses to love. Rejecting complex patterns of symbolism or imagery, he relied on the rhetoric of song: the repetition of evocative lines, the direct, earnest declaration of love, the musical cadence of simple meter and rhyme. The consequent subtlety resides not in his meaning, but in the delicacy of his emotional touch, his ability to choose the appropriate vehicle for the mood he wishes to re-create in us. Even where there is an apparent theme, as in "The Poet's Love," the statement is often only a measurement of the depth of his present bitterness or pleasure. No matter how objective or thematic the language may appear, the force behind the song is always Clare's personal situation and mood.

IV *Lyrics*

The difference between a song and a lyric in Clare's work is often a matter more of degree than kind. Although at their furthest remove his lyrics are complex, philosophical, and on occasion profound, many of his more restrained lyrics border on the simplicity of song. It is necessary to define the boundary between song and lyric, not for the sake of adding to the

literature of generic distinctions, but to demonstrate the
diversity of Clare's method, a method which allowed him to
explore his intricate, often ambivalent, responses to love, nature,
and his own personality, but which remained firmly rooted in the
musical cadences and verbal austerity of his songs. Clare never
lost—on the contrary, in his later years he seems to have
reaffirmed—that striving for compression, precision, and direct
communication that inspired his most artless songs. The escala-
tion of complexity in metrical arrangement and subject matter
was not a chronological one so much as a concurrent response to
different levels of feeling. While content at times to limit himself
to the conventional expressions of emotion, even of passions that
were originally personal in their impact on him, he strove at
other times to penetrate the intensity of his emotional
experience, to reproduce unique expressions of the profound
insights he gained from his own particular circumstances.

Near the boundary between song and lyric we find several
poems that have superficial qualities of song but that add a
subtlety, both in metrical variation and in imagery, which is
always extraneous to pure song. Clare's imagery in his songs
seldom distracts us from the direct communication of his
feelings. Occasionally individual images draw our attention as
they do in these lines from "Her I Love":

> When Pulpy Plums to ripeness swells
> In down surrounding blue
> When dews besprent on Heather Bells
> Reflecting brighter hue.[40]

Or this from a fragment in manuscript: "Crimson with awes the
whitethorn bends."[41] But this originality rarely occurs in those
verses that otherwise adhere to the true spirit of song. Clare
learned the value of simplicity from the Scottish songwriters
whom he admired: "the Scotch poets excell in song-writing
because they take their images from common life where nature
exists without affectation."[42] In his own songs conventional
epithets exist alongside simple unadorned images from nature.

In the lyrics, however, Clare's imagery often exerts a subtle
pressure on the narrative or lyrical statement of the poem,
slightly altering our first impression of his meaning. This

phenomenon is perhaps an extension of the tendency in many of
his songs to invoke the aid of nature in convincing his lover to
meet him or to return his love. But in the more complex lyrics a
greater originality marks this use of imagery. In "A Whimpering
Brook," for example, Clare utilizes the weight of natural imagery
to establish the precise time both of the year and of the day in
which he would like to meet Lucy. The smell of hay and clover in
the first stanza emphasizes the summer season, and the precision
of detail in the second and third identifies the exact point in the
evening which he thinks will be most propitious to his courting:

> The white moth flits upon the wing
> The bat has left the willow tree
> In brook banks chittering crickets sing
> Come Lucy dear and walk with me.[43]

Further detail built up around the concept of time leads us to
believe that the meeting will fail of its full enjoyment if the
precise moment is not taken advantage of. This transience is
further emphasized by contrast with the constancy of the old
oak, "still standing in its ancient place." All this imagery reflects
a sense of urgency, a feeling that the conditions he makes are so
difficult to meet that the time may be missed. The invitation is
left characteristically unresolved; the time has not come; Lucy's
arrival is uncertain. The foreboding imagery itself suggests the
wishful thinking that Clare is indulging in. There is even a hint in
the final stanza that he finds some compensation for her absence
in the simple contemplation of the scene itself:

> The unseen shower of falling dew
> How sweet we meet its fall at eve
> When every thing perks up anew
> And fancy pleasing visions wave
> Its eve song as the cricket sung
> Snug in its moss nest sleeps the bee
> The ground lark broods on eggs and young
> Come Lucy wander out with me.

A similar urgency emerges from the imagery in "Lines—to
Helen Maria" where the transience of life in autumn is used as an
argument to hasten Helen's meeting with him:

> Helen Maria! lovely Helen!
> Ere the foliage leaves the tree
> Ere the snow storm hides the dwelling,
> Take a country walk with me.[44]

But a more intricate example of the pressure Clare's details exert
on the interpretation of a lyric is "Mary Helen from the Hill."
With its conventional heroine, regular meter, and simple diction,
it bears a superficial resemblance to a number of Clare's songs.
But a closer analysis reveals the unequal length of the three
stanzas, a preponderance of description, and a total lack of
emotional rhetoric. In fact, it is a delicately suggestive lyric
expressing a subtle foreboding rather than an overt declaration
of love. The first stanza describes the setting in which Mary
Helen is accustomed to walk:

> The flaggy wheat is in the ear
> At the low end of the town
> And the barley horns begin to spear
> Fine the spindle through the crown
> The black snail he has crept abroad
> In dangers ways to run
> And midges oer the road
> Are dancing in the sun
> When firdales darkest shadows leave
> Sweet Mary Hellen walks at eve.[45]

This appears the height of objectivity, giving us no indication of
the poet's relationship with the girl and little revelation of his
feeling toward her. She is, simply, sweet. What attracts our
attention is the detail surrounding her. It establishes the time of
year and time of day that Mary Helen walks and it evokes the
transience of the moment by accenting the continuous development of the wheat and barley. It also brings to our attention the
dancing of the midges and the parallel between the black snail
and Mary Helen, both venturing abroad in the evening. This
association would perhaps be less striking if Mary Helen were
not also linked with the "darkest shadows" cast by the fir trees.
By the end of the stanza she is clearly associated in Clare's mind
with darkness.

The second stanza immediately reinforces these ominous
connotations by adding the concepts of depth and danger:

> In the deep dyke grows the reed
> The bullrush wabbles deeper still
> And oval leaves of water weed
> The dangerous deeper places fill
> The river winds and feels no ill
> How lovely sinks the setting sun
> The fish leaps up with trembling trill
> Grasshoppers chirrup on the reed
> The mead so green the air so still
> Evening assembles sweet indeed
> With Mary Hellen from the Hill
> Who wanders by that rivers brim
> In dewy flowers and shadows dim.

Clare has set up, in an ostensibly innocent background description, a contrast between the surface picture of sunset, leaping fish, grasshoppers, and dancing midges—the world of carefree activity in which Mary Helen walks—and the submerged world of mystery and danger. The river "feels" no ill, but the very mention of possible ill, however unfelt, adds to the sinister atmosphere of the poem. And we are left at the conclusion of this middle stanza with another parallel, this one between Mary and the river. Both wander, but although the river "feels no ill," Mary, who is presumably equally sanguine, is again in the shadows.

The final stanza returns to the surface world, but with constant reminders of the presence of the river:

> Right merrily the midges dance
> Above the river stream
> Their wings like silver atoms glance
> In evenings golden beam
> The boat track by the rivers side
> Where Mary Hellen roves
> The cloud sky when the river wide
> The banks o willow groves
> And Mary Hellen in young pride
> Rambling by the river side.

Now the midges dance above the river, emphasizing the contrast between the gay activities on the surface and the danger underneath. Otherwise the suggestive power of Clare's imagery is essentially submerged. Only with the repeated references to the river and the single phrase describing Mary "in young pride" are we reminded of the sinister overtones of the previous stanzas. But they are ineradicably there, and Mary Helen in her confident youth is unaware of the dangers which lurk about her. The poem is nicely suggestive at the end. No immediate harm is forecast for the girl in the shadows—who is herself a shadowy figure in the poem—but the possibility is there, and is hidden from her. In the longer run, the poem suggests, the dancing, leaping, rambling activity of life above the surface must come to terms with the "dangerous deeper places." But the uncertainty at the end is also effective because it does not presume, as I have done, to judge. It simply establishes the dichotomy between two aspects of our existence and places the girl in that context. The fact that she is young adds the further element of progression, the suspicions about her future relationship to that dichotomy. Her relationship to the poet loses interest to us because of the powerfully suggestive context of imagery in which we find her. She is last seen wandering in close proximity to the river.

A more overt, expressly philosophical, relationship between imagery and theme controls "The Dying Child," one of the most sensitive expressions we have of Clare's personal insight into the natural order. The logic here, established in the opening stanza, works on the juxtaposition of concepts we instinctively feel to be appropriate, although rationally suspect:

> He could not die when trees were green
> For he loved the time too well
> His little hands when flowers were seen
> Was held for the blue-bell
> As he was carried o'er the green.[46]

The two sentences that comprise this stanza are self-contained but their juxtaposition suggests a causal connection between the phenomena they describe. More corroboration is added in stanza two:

> His eye glanced at the white-nosed bee
> He knew those children of the spring
> When he was well and on the lea
> He held one in his hands to sing
> Which filled his little heart with glee.

The poet's analysis of the child's situation, interjected in the third stanza, is contained in a query, signifying his own uncertainty about justice in the natural order:

> Infants, the children of the spring
>   How can an infant die
> When butterflies are on the wing
>   Green grass, and such a sky
>   How can an infant die at spring.

Behind this questioning is the agony of knowledge that children do die in the prime of life and in the most pleasant season of the year. The harmony the poet finds so satisfying in this child's life and death implies, by inversion, the injustice experienced by others. The final three stanzas describe the progressive deterioration of the child's health, paralleling the movement from spring and summer to winter:

> He held his hand for daiseys white
>   And then for violets blue
> And took them all to bed at night
>   That in the green fields grew
>   As childhoods sweet delight
>
> And then he shut his little eyes
>   And flowers would notice not
> Birds nests and eggs, made no surprise
>   Nor any blossoms got
>   They met with plantive sighs
>
> When winter came and blasts did sigh
>   And bare was plain and tree
> As he for ease in bed did lie
>   His soul seemed with the free
>   He died so quietly.

A cluster of natural images reinforces the appropriateness of the child's death, providing a measure of consolation to the poet because he sees the semblance of a natural order at work in the child's life. The abundant spring and summer imagery corresponds to the child's full life; its eventual barrenness in the final stanza signifies his death. With what has become known as Blakean mysticism Clare finds a particular power in this child's relationship with his natural environment, which allows him to die within the natural cycle. Clare seems to feel at least a partial reassurance that a natural order exists, even if he begs the question of the child dying at all and implies the knowledge that other children are not so fortunate in the circumstances of their death. What is important, however, is the momentary insight, vulnerable as it may be to later rationalization. That insight is the sign of a lyrical poet, not simply a songwriter.

The contrast between life and death in this poem derives its force from the vivid color of the imagery. Clare does not rely on objects which are associated with particular colors, but on the repeated, explicit naming of the color he wants to evoke. The green of trees and grass is specifically mentioned, even accented by his use of "green" as a noun to unite all our sensations of healthy nature into a single image—an image, incidentally, that Blake used with symbolic effect in *Songs of Innocence*. Similarly, Clare stresses the blue of the flowers (again through a noun, "bluebell," as well as an adjective, "violets blue") and the white of bee and daisy. The final stanza is notably devoid of color. The less evocative term "plain" is substituted for "green" when describing the location of the child's former activity, and the tree and green are bare.

As Clare was himself increasingly estranged from the beauties of nature, either physically because of declining health or spiritually because of the depression of his later years, his imagery followed a corresponding shift to the unnatural and surreal. Distortion of natural imagery became a predominant feature of the late lyrics, nowhere used with as consummate skill as in "An Invite to Eternity."

Echoes of Marlowe's "The Passionate Shepherd to His Love" in this poem accompany an invitation that is anything but pastoral. Clare's idealism has been shattered; his close identification with nature, once the most positive force behind his view of the world, is now altered into a purgatorial vision of a threatening afterlife:

> Wilt thou go with me sweet maid
> Say maiden wilt thou go with me
> Through the valley depths of shade
> Of night and dark obscurity
> Where the path hath lost its way

Where the sun forgets the day
Where there's nor life nor light to see
Sweet maiden wilt thou go with me

Where stones will turn to flooding streams
Where plains will rise like ocean waves
Where life will fade like visioned dreams
And mountains darken into caves
Say maiden wilt thou go with me
Through this sad non-identity
Where parents live and are forgot
And sisters live and know us not

Say maiden wilt thou go with me
In this strange death of life to be
To live in death and be the same
Without this life or home or name
At once to be and not to be
That was and is not—yet to see
Things pass like shadows—and the sky
Above, below, around us lie.

The land of shadows wilt thou trace
And look nor know each others face
The present mixed with reasons gone
And past and present all as one
Say maiden can thy life be led
To join the living with the dead
Then trace thy footsteps on with me
We're wed to one eternity.[47]

Here Clare's obscure and surreal imagery reinforces his theme
by reflecting the uncertainty of his own future. Nature, like his
identity, will be in a state of transition with rocks turning into
water, plains into oceans, and mountains into caves. The life-in-
death he envisages, suspended in the sky and confused between
a Christian Heaven and the world of nightmares, is not radically
different from his present life in the asylum where he is also cut
off from family and friends, without home or social status. With
no personal illusions about release through death, he asks for the
ultimate dedication from his companion, offering in return only a
path that has "lost its way."
    The later lyrics also reveal an increasingly stark use of images

describing women. The absence of natural imagery in the
following poem, ostensibly about past love, is itself significant
when we remember the scores of similar lyrics extolling the
inseparability of woman and nature. These "Stanzas" successfully re-create the mood of uncertainty which accompanies
Clare's attempt to remember the personality of a former lover.
In the first stanza the images of blackness and the "angry blast"
are mingled with a succession of faces out of which he cannot
catch a recollection of her former smile:

> Black absence hides upon the past
>   I quite forget thy face
> And memory like the angry blast
>   Will love's last smile erace
> I try to think of what has been
>   But all is blank to me
> And other faces pass between
> My early love and thee.[48]

The imagery of violence is supported by the abrupt syntactical
change between lines one and two, and the curious mixture of
sibilants and plosives in the whole stanza. Both result from the
frustration of the speaker at the impotence both of memory and,
more particularly, of his personal mental state which is incapable
of recapturing past emotion. This latter problem is outlined in
the second stanza where the speaker acknowledges his ability to
recall physical details of the woman—thus admitting to some
powers of memory—but cannot penetrate beyond them to the
recollection of either her personality or the passion he previously felt for her:

> I try to trace thy memory now
>   And only find thy name
> Those inky lashes on thy brow
>   Black hair, and eyes the same
> Thy round pale face of snowy dyes
>   There's nothing paints thee there
> A darkness comes before my eyes
> For nothing seems so fair.

The inadequacy of the mind to resurrect the past is superbly
evoked by the "black and white" imagery throughout the entire

poem. Memory deals in outlines—"inky lashes," "black hair and eyes" on a "pale face." The past is blank and dark; the outline of his former lover's physical features stands out as if in a monochrome photograph or charcoal sketch. In the final stanza he reiterates his frustration, again using the stark imagery of the previous stanzas. But he now reveals his own suppression which has forced the image into his mind. Her name has been a "hidden thought"; their contact has been a vicarious one. He is trying to recapture a relationship that never really existed:

> I knew thy name so sweet and young
> 'Twas music to my ears
> A silent word upon my tongue
> A hidden thought for years
> Dark hair and lashes swarthy too
> Arched on thy forehead pale
> All else is vanished from my view
> Like voices on the gale.

It is appropriate that he is left with only a physical memory; the "all else" which has vanished was never known intimately. The imagery controls the poem, giving it an atmosphere entirely consistent with the mental phenomenon it explores. Our rather nightmarish response to his situation arises from the absence of color images, from the stark contrast between the pale face in the dark recesses of the memory, and the dark hair and lashes which accent it. Even the aural imagery contributes to the mood. The angry blast of the opening stanza returns in the final simile of the poem where the apparition of her face is likened to a single lingering memory of sound after the other sounds have been wiped out by the storm. This is one of Clare's most haunting lyrics, not essentially concerned with vanished love as so many of them are, but with recreating a vision of the inadequacy of the mind to retain experience.

A similarly introspective series of lyrics explores Clare's growing preoccupation with his position in the world, as both a man and a poet. These lyrics are as obscure in their literal meaning as they are mystical in their expression, but they carry a certain power which makes them the most often anthologized of Clare's works. In them we find a different Clare from the sensitive lover of nature and woman. Here is an often defiant,

always misunderstood poet concerned about his personal relationship with the world outside the asylum. He attempts, usually
through overstatement, to convince the world of his stature as
poet and man. Consequently, he loses the intimacy that comes
from a direct address to a lover or an individual reader. In these
poems he addresses the world at large in grand, sweeping
rhetoric designed to overwhelm rather than seduce.

   Some of these lyrics are argumentative. They attempt to
persuade the reader either that poets have been victimized by
their society or that Clare himself is worthy of greater
consideration than he has received. "The Poet's Song" is one of
the quieter, more restrained of these lyrics, listing three groups
in society which have their own comforts in life and concluding
with an abrupt summation of the poet's lot:

> The maid has beauty at her will
>   Too often flung away
> And broken down and lovely still
>   O who would betray
>
> The wealthy have their wealth and power
>   And almost all the world to spend
> They seldom know a weary hour
>   And favour never wants a friend
>
> The many have a home retreat
>   To while away a weary hour
> The poorest have a corner seat
>   And only covet wealth and power
>
> Despised and hated all along
> The bard has nothing but a song.[49]

The bitterness concentrated in the last stanza shocks the reader
who has been lulled into complacency by the truisms of the
previous stanzas. It is reinforced by the change to a single
couplet from the more expansive alternating rhyme of the
quatrains. The true extent of his bitterness is felt when we
consider the compensation he sees other groups receiving. The
poem implies he would feel compensated for the misery of life if
he were a jaded beauty, if his friends were faithful because of his
money, or if he was poor and idle. Ultimately his logic falters

because of these examples and we are left with the impression that his extreme dejection has marred his ability to see his position in a balanced perspective.

Several other poems of this type sacrifice the intelligibility of "The Poet's Song" for a mystical intensity which twentieth-century readers tend to admire in spite of the resulting obscurity. "A Vision," for example, is virtually incomprehensible even if we grant it the appeal of its flamboyant imagery and sweeping rhetoric:

> I lost the love of heaven above
> I spurned the lust of earth below
> I felt the sweets of fancied love
> And hell itself my only foe
>
> I lost earth's joys but felt the flow
> Of heaven's flame abound in me
> Till loveliness and I did grow
> The bard of immortality
>
> I loved but woman fell away
> I hid me from her faded fame
> I snatched the sun's eternal ray
> And wrote till earth was but a name
>
> In every language upon earth
> On every shore o'er every sea,
> I gave my name immortal birth,
> And kept my spirit with the free.[50]

We can appreciate the rather effective contrasts between heavenly love and earthly lust, and even the inconsistency inherent in lines one and six can be explained as a loss and regaining of his favor with God. But the blatant hyperbole of his claim to have been "the bard of immortality" and the falsity of the final stanza belie what elements of truth we find in the poem. His pathetic attempt to convince us of this freedom and immortality denies the veracity of his assertion. If his claim is true, such an inflated statement of it is unnecessary.

The weaknesses of this poem permeate most of his "mystical" lyrics, leaving many of them impossible to understand. But a few, especially "The Peasant Poet," combine Clare's sensitivity to

nature with his stark view of the world from the confinement of
the asylum. The details here are all explicable, all contributing to
a self-assessment that reveals Clare's true claim to our attention:

> He loved the brook's soft sound
> The swallow swimming by
> He loved the daisy coverd ground
> The cloud bedappled sky
> To him the dismal storm appeared
> The very voice of God
> And where the Evening rock was reared
> Stood Moses with his rod
> And every thing his eyes surveyed
> The insects i' the brake
> Where creatures God almighty made
> He loved them for his sake
> A silent man in lifes affairs
> A thinker from a Boy
> A Peasant in his daily cares—
> The Poet in his joy.[51]

The third person speaker and his use of the past tense give the
poem the air of an epitaph. A tone of confidence and satisfaction
emanates from the description and from the positive note on
which the poem ends. This conclusion has been prepared by the
earlier description of Clare's attitude to nature in her various
moods, an attitude which appropriately occupies the major
portion of his life summary. The final four lines contain Clare's
most succinct and accurate self-assessment. And they rightly
give the predominant position to Clare's poetic life. Poetry was
only one facet of his life, but it was the important one, the aspect
which gave him what joy he was able to find to transcend the
difficult situation into which he was born. The shift from "a" to
"the" in the last line emphasizes the awe with which Clare
viewed his own powers.

This poem displays a technical competence characteristic of
Clare's best lyrics, too. After the two opening trimeter lines with
their evocative sibilants suggesting the murmur of the brook and
the swallow, the poem moves in alternating tetrameter and
trimeter lines. The effect of this alternation is to give in the
shorter line a sense of completion after the length of the
tetrameter line. Combining with the line length is a pattern of

repeated syntactical structures and individual words. The repetition of "he loved" in the first four lines combined with the increased length of line three and the return to trimeter in line four gives a sense of rhetorical climax and return to the normal flow of his verse. The subsequent eight lines are held together by coordinate conjunctions and, presumably, a semicolon at the end of line eleven. The concluding four lines not only escalate to the climactic final assertion of joy in poetry, but suggest through the alternating line lengths a balance between the two pairs of personal attributes. He is a silent man and a thinker, a peasant and a poet. The effect of these final lines is further enhanced by the ambiguity of tense. The previous lines are clearly in the past tense, but the lack of a verb in the final lines, with its resulting lack of tense, applies his assessment not only to the past but also to the present. This is an epitaph, but also a statement of his present creed.

The obscurity that mars many of Clare's other late asylum lyrics may have resulted from the deterioration of his mental faculties, but it could, equally as plausibly, have been the consequence of the increasing futility of attempting to communicate with a world that no longer recognized his existence. The hope of future publication which sustained his poetic powers before and immediately after his incarceration must have receded with every additional year spent at Northampton. Without an audience, the inspiration to speak directly and intelligibly was inevitably weakened. The poems produced under these conditions reveal a mind gradually retreating into the wilderness of private symbolism without leaving the signposts necessary for us to follow.

CHAPTER 6

Child Harold

NO single poem of Clare's has suffered from editorial indiscretions to quite the extent *Child Harold* has. Written six years after *The Rural Muse* (1835), the last volume of poetry he published during his life, this, the most original of his long poems, did not appear in print until J. W. Tibble's *The Poems of John Clare*, nearly a century later. Even then the material from Clare's manuscripts was rearranged into a series of separate poems and songs without acknowledging their original contribution to a larger single work. Fourteen years later, having omitted almost all of the songs and removed all but one of the remainder from the stanzaic framework, Geoffrey Grigson printed the stanzas of *Child Harold* as a single, albeit mutilated, poem.[1] Not until 1964, in Eric Robinson and Geoffrey Summerfield's *The Later Poems of John Clare*, was the poem published in a form that respected the arrangement of songs and stanzas we find in Clare's notebooks.[2]

The main source all editors have drawn upon is a foolscap notebook into which Clare copied a revised version of previously composed *Child Harold* material during the months he spent at home after his escape from High Beech in July, 1841. Here the poem is interspersed with verses from *Don Juan*, paraphrases of the Bible, and miscellaneous passages of prose. Clare himself drew from several earlier sources for the version that appears in this fair-copy notebook. His primary source was another notebook which he used at High Beech to compose, again interspersed with other material, drafts of stanzas and songs for *Don Juan* and *Child Harold*. Other, briefer jottings for the poem appear in one of his scrapbooks, on the cover of an exercise book inscribed "Wm Clare 19 April 1841," in another notebook that Clare was using during the autumn and winter of 1841, in an exercise book which also contains "Tis Martinmass from Rig to

Rig," and in the margins of two newspapers, the *Lincolnshire Chronicle* (Aug 27, 1841) and the *Lincoln, Rutland and Stamford Mercury* (Sept 3, 1841).[3] Other verses appear for the first time, as far as we can tell, in the fair-copy notebook. Collating this wealth of material is not a simple task—although the most reliable text derives from the least complex approach to Clare's originals—but it is necessary for an understanding of Clare's most difficult, but also most rewarding, long poem.

As a result of its erratic editorial history *Child Harold's* critical reception has been recent and brief, marked by the inevitable confusion of any commentary which is based on unreliable texts. The variety of responses the poem has provoked owes as much to the several forms in which it appeared as to its undoubted richness of content and technique. Grigson's editorial assumptions govern his pioneering critical statements about the poem; noticing the motif of changing seasons, he crystallizes it into a complete structure for the poem. Clare, he believes,

seems to have planned it as a poem of four cantos. Two cantos were finished before his return, and the second of them a spring and summer canto. At Northborough he wrote a canto for the autumn. He added one stanza beginning " 'Tis winter and the fields are bare and waste", and there the poem may have been interrupted by his removal to Northampton.[4]

Apart from Clare's rather loose use of the term "canto" in his letters, however, no evidence has appeared to support Grigson's contention, nor does Clare's sequence of stanzas and songs in the fair-copy notebook justify Grigson's rearrangement. What this notebook does support, though, is Grigson's observations that after his initial breakdown Clare "was still able to carry the impulse to a single poem—and a long one—through several days."[5]

Clare's poetical stamina also impressed Naomi Lewis. With access to Tibble's and Grigson's versions only, she praised *Child Harold* as a "long, sustained, intricate poem."[6] Although she does not follow this statement with any substantial analysis, she finds in *Child Harold* "some of the most notable lyrical writing in the language."[7] Fortunately, both these comments ignore the structure of the poem, focusing instead on impressions that an accumulation of stanzas can provide. Not until the publication of

Robinson and Summerfield's version, following Clare's own arrangement of the stanzas and songs, was a structural approach possible. They themselves found that although *Child Harold* "is not in the first place a unity," it is "more sustained in thought than anything else he ever attempted."[8]

The first lengthy discussion of the reliable text of the poem, in Mark Storey's *The Poetry of John Clare,* stresses its biographical importance, calling it "the fullest picture of Clare the suffering man that we have, apart from his prose and letters." Viewing it as "a hybrid poem of near-madness," Storey finds it "a pathetic poem, one to which it is particularly difficult (and perhaps inapposite) to apply the usual critical responses." "There is cohesion of sorts," he admits, "but as a whole the poem lacks structure and polish."[9] There *is* structure to *Child Harold,* though, and Storey himself hints at its character. He acknowledges, for example, that "some unity is imposed by a skilful use of patterns of imagery and by the careful deployment of varying stanzaic forms. But the spirit of the poem is largely one of changing moods, of contrasts and oppositions."[10] If he had meant "structure" rather than "spirit," and if he had noticed these moods governing the total orchestration of the poem, as well as the local alternations between song and stanza that he does mention, we would have a clearer idea of the poem's form. For the richness of *Child Harold,* its sustained but infinitely varied lyrical impulse, the extremities of emotional experience it relates, and the tone of near-madness Storey finds in it, are controlled by an intricately woven pattern of formal devices. At least three of these devices are worth looking at, not only to amplify what previous critics have noticed, but also to demonstrate the larger principle of organization they seem to have missed.

The most immediately noticeable of these devices is the tension created between the subjective outbursts of passion which characterize the songs, and the more objective, distanced stanzas which attempt to explain the basis of these passions. We are seldom given direct links between the two dominant types of verse; what we are given is a relationship based on juxtaposition. The songs are more integral to the total effect of the poem than Grigson would have us believe when he misreads them as attempts "to lighten [*Child Harold*] as Byron had lightened the length of his poem, with songs."[11] True, some of Clare's songs have that effect, but the majority of them are songs of anguish, direct expressions of the pain Clare feels at the loss of his home and his early love. They are counterbalanced, on the other hand, by the stanzas' attempt to explain, rather than express; to come to terms with, rather than to sing, the peculiar experiences that have contributed to Clare's emotional life. Between song and stanza there is often a tenuous thematic link, but more often the tension derives from a subjective expression of a particular mood juxtaposed with a more objective attempt at personal assessment.

Storey bases his view of the poem's structure on a second formal device, patterns of imagery. He points out a series of contrasting motifs: sunrise and sunset, light and dark, storm and calm, and prison and freedom. Such a pattern reflects Clare's vacillating states of mind and, through gradual movement from one side of each dichotomy to another, something of the progress of Clare's emotional development in the poem. We can add to these another pair of images, too, one that controls the progress of the poem, giving it a definite sense of development.

Although this imagery, of the enveloping forest and its opposite, the exposing fen, is introduced in the first song of *Child Harold*, where both images prove that "Nature's love is eternal,"[12] its dominance emerges in the stanzas, where we begin to see Clare's propensity to convert the immediate landscape into the image patterns that characterize his mature poetry. His walks in the forested environs of High Beech asylum provide him with an image appropriate to his theme of consolation in bondage:

> The sun has gone down with a veil on her brow
> While I in the forest sit museing alone
> The maiden has been oer the hills for her cow
> While my hearts affections are freezing to stone.

Elsewhere in *Child Harold* confinement in the asylum brings to his mind images of iron chains, but he finds in the enveloping beeches a more comforting restriction:

> Nor will I repine though in love we're divided
> She in the Lowlands and I in the glen
> Of these forest beeches—by nature we're guided
> And I shall find rest on her bosom agen.

Throughout the early part of the poem Clare stresses an affinity
with the forest, an ability to find in it a compensation for the
absence of his beloved Mary:

> How beautiful this hill of fern swells on
> So beautifull the chappel peeps between
> The hornbeams—with its simple bell—alone
> I wander here hid in a palace green
> Mary is abscent—but the forest queen
> Nature is with me—morning noon and gloaming
> I write my poems in these paths unseen
> And when among these brakes and beeches roaming
> I sigh for truth and home and love and woman.

Even the hint of mythology in "forest queen" cannot distract
from Clare's intensely personal view of the forest. While it
enforces a form of bondage, cutting him off from the outside
world, it also reassures him that his confinement is endurable. He
is subject not to the agony suggested by physical chains, but to
the enveloping compensation of omnipresent nature. The
complexity of his response to the asylum, which isolated him
from those he loved but at the same time allowed personal
communion with nature, is admirably captured in the forest
image.

The middle of the poem, dominated by Clare's mental and
emotional search for Mary, uses as its focus the image of the plain
or fen. Freed from the confinement of the forest he is also
stripped of the security he found in it. He is now exposed, searching for a woman who has already died physically but whose
memory influences the poet's every utterance. Her former
presence pervades the plain, giving it its significance in the
poem: "e'en these fens where wood nor grove / Are seen—their
very nakedness I love / For one dwells nigh that secret hopes
prefer."[13] Unlike the forest which gave him reassurance, the fen
by its intimacy with Mary and its failure to reveal her
whereabouts, and in spite of his love for the fen landscape,
provides a rebuke and a relentless message that his hopes for a
reunion with Mary are futile:

> I've sought her in the fields and flowers
> I've sought her in the forest groves
> In avanues and shaded bowers

> And every scene that Mary loves
> E'en round her home I seek her here
> But Mary's abscent every where.[14]

Whereas the forest assured him that the beneficence of nature was everywhere, the fens—ironically void of obstructions to his physical vision—expose the truth not only that he and Mary are separated but that her absence is final, is "every where." His love for this landscape is ultimately based, therefore, on its being the scene of his former relationship with her.

In the last stanzas of the poem—as we have it, without Clare's final arrangement—the forest image reemerges. Clare returns to the theme of freedom in bondage that characterized his earlier image of the forest. Now, in a "shadey Grove," he acknowledges that "my prison is a spring to me" and that "my very bondage though in snares—is free." What is merely a grove in that stanza escalates to a "green wood" in the next and finally to a forest in the succeeding stanza:

> Wrecked of all hopes save one to be alone
> Where Solitude becomes my wedded mate
> Sweet Forest with rich beauties overgrown
> Where solitude is queen and riegns in state
> Hid in green trees I hear the clapping gate
> And voices calling to the rambling cows
> I Laugh at Love and all its idle fate
> The present hour is all my lot allows
> An age of sorrow springs from lovers vows.

Echoes of the first references to the forest, in the "fern hill" stanza, reinforce the structural symmetry of Clare's progress through the poem. The references to a queen in the forest, to solitude, and to being "hid" in the "green" of the forest unite the later with the earlier passage. Clare has returned to a position approximating that from which he started, but the difference in tone between these stanzas indicates what impact the intervening emotional experiences have had on him. The sigh in the former passage is replaced by a laugh in the latter. This defiant note is strengthened rather than softened by its relationship to the imagery; he laughs from the security of solitude, but the failure of the forest, and everything he has embodied in it, to compensate for the loss of Mary, is implicit in his laugh.

Clare's return to the image of the forest demonstrates his command of the technique of distilling images from nature that he describes in his comments on the poetic process. Clare confirms, in an unmailed letter to Mary Joyce, that the forest was literally the setting in which parts of the poem were written: "I went a few evenings on Fern Hill & wrote a new Canto of 'Child Harold' & now I am better."[15] But by the end of the poem it has become symbolic, too, depending as much for effect on our memory of its earlier use as on its original purpose of identifying the physical location. As a symbol unique to this poem the forest provides unity in a way that cannot be done by the sun, which is a general image in Clare's work, or by the metaphor of a ship at sea, which remains an impersonal cliché in *Child Harold*.

A third, more integral, principle of organization is the orchestration of tones and moods which gives us the sense of form unfolding as we read. The poem chronicles Clare's emotional turbulence during one of the most severe crises in his crisis-ridden life, revealing his mind with frightening lucidity in moods ranging from anguish to ecstasy. But it would be dangerous to exaggerate the biographical elements in the poem's organization, thereby running the risk of reducing the poem to a record of the poet's response to asylum life and to his subsequent escape into the outside world. A comparison of Clare's last draft of *Child Harold* with the notebooks containing the original jottings reveals Clare's deliberate attempt to give form to the poem, to arrange his lyrical outbursts and contemplative stanzas into an organic whole rather than a chronological record. The form he chose is a continuous one—he did not divide the poem into distinct sections—but within it are clearly recognizable units each characterized by a dominant mood. While it is unlikely that he consciously arranged his work to resemble a symphony, a comparison with that musical form will be illuminating in describing the kind of form Clare imposed on his material. Each unit, for example, is governed by a single, though often complex, mood, but within the unit there are variations of tone and movement from one nuance to another. Through the course of the poem, too, these units are arranged to create a clear sense of progression from mood to mood. As with a symphony, our submission to the movements and their orchestration is requisite to a rewarding aesthetic experience.

On this principle *Child Harold* contains nine "movements." If

Clare had completed his revision of the final third of the poem, the structure might have been altered, but even as it stands now that final third is remarkably unified. Each new movement is marked by a clear change in tone between its first stanza and the conclusion of the previous section. Section One, for example, ends with Clare resigned to his solitude but nostalgic for previous lovers: "for I've been roaming / With both at morn and noon and dusky gloaming."[16] Section Two abruptly changes the tone: "Cares gather round I snap their chains in two / And smile in agony and laugh in tears." The stanzas that follow continue, with variations, this new tone of violence and surreality.

By comparing early drafts with Clare's last *Child Harold* manuscript we can see the evidence of his creating a sequence of moods out of the chronologically composed original. The first section, comprised of the initial eleven stanzas and the four songs interspersed with them, is arranged from two earlier manuscripts. The opening stanza and first song seem always to have been intended to open the poem—they open the earlier draft as well—but the remainder of the section is significantly rearranged. Most of it was written at High Beech before Clare's escape and return to Northborough, but the second stanza and two of the songs, "I've Wandered Many a Weary Mile" and "Here's Where Mary Loved to Be," where composed after his return. Both songs appear relatively early in the section, preceding several stanzas that were actually written before them. Another song, "Sweet Days While God Your Blessings Send," although written at the same time as "Here's Where Mary Loved to Be," does not appear until much later in the poem, in Section Three. In fact, only stanzas five to eleven remain in the same sequence in the fair-copy manuscript as they appear in the High Beech notebook.

The break between Sections One and Two illustrates Clare's method. The first stanza of the second section, containing the abrupt change of mood already mentioned, is in fact the final one in the sequence of stanzas that ends the previous section. The remaining stanzas and songs are gathered from a number of sources to provide variations on the violent mood of that stanza. He takes the song "Written in a Thunder storm," composed at the asylum on July 15, 1841, from near the front of the High Beech notebook and follows it with a stanza written after July 24, the date of his return to Northborough. That stanza in turn is followed by one of several stanzas originally jotted down in the "Wm. Clare" scrapbook. Only then do we finally read the three stanzas which come after the first stanza and song of the original arrangement in the High Beech notebook. The subsequent three stanzas in the final version are not found in any of the existing manuscripts; it is not impossible they were composed on the spot to suit the mood he was expanding in this section. The movement concludes with a pair of songs, one taken from the area of the High Beech manuscript immediately after Clare's account of his return, and the other from the very end of the same manuscript.

Clearly, then, Clare "composed" this piece, selecting stanzas and songs from various previously written manuscripts to satisfy the principle of organization he had in mind. The remaining sections of the poem demonstrate a similarly meticulous rearrangement, except for what I have chosen to treat as the final section. Clare ceased rearranging after the forty-eighth stanza after which our most reliable source for Clare's projected poem is its sequence in the High Beech notebook. As we will see later, this long section has remarkable unity as it stands. But we must be careful not to accord it the same quality of completion that we do the earlier ones. We are not relying totally on speculation, however, as Clare numbered the stanzas in this section, perhaps as a preliminary step to copying them into the fair-copy notebook. Furthermore, since Clare did not extract a single stanza from his long sequence for use in other parts of the poem, we can safely assume that he considered these stanzas a reasonably coherent unit.

As the poem appears in Robinson and Summerfield's edition it is an impressive, compelling arrangement of moods and their variations which leads from an initial self-confidence, in the face of bewildering adversity, to a final attitude of resignation partially belied by an impulse toward defiance. The passions Clare examines are not simple ones—not easily reduced to an adjective or two—but are the genuine, complex, often contradictory emotions of a man whose position in society and literature appears increasingly tenuous, continually threatened by the indifference of those to whom he tries to speak. They spring from the anguish, not so much of an imbalanced mind, as of a sensitive imagination viewing a world which has inexplicably rejected it, certifying it unfit for normal human intercourse after admiring its earlier poetic effusions. A major part of Clare's success in reconciling these apparent contradictions depends on his principle of organization, his creation of mood and tone, rather than his manipulation of more tangible literary devices, to hold his poem together. His temporary intellectual certainties are repeatedly subjected to contradiction in his moments of emotional insight—his stanzas are often modified by his songs— but both are subordinated to the general flow of moods and local movements of tone.

The predominant tone of the first section is of a tenuous but persistent confidence that the poet's current predicament can be overcome by contact with nature or by union with Mary after death.[17] The poem begins with a firm assertion of the ideal role of a poet—"Real poets must be truly honest men"—juxtaposed in the same stanza with an endorsement of rural life—"The life of labour is a rural song." This declamatory opening establishes the formal, objective attitude that will predominate in the poem's stanzas and is immediately counterbalanced by an intimate examination of personal experience in the opening song. Here the consolation Clare finds in the surrounding forest is sufficient to keep his potential indignation in check:

> For homes and friends vanished
> I have kindness not wrath
> For in days care has banished
> My heart possessed both
>
> My hopes are all hopeless
> My skys have no sun
> Winter fell in youths mayday
> And still freezes on
>
> But Love like the seed is
> In the heart of a flower
> It will blossom with truth
> In a prosperous hour.

"Kindness not wrath" is the key expression here. It captures the tone of the entire section. Even when his calm self-assurance and refusal to succumb to anger descend almost to despair in the song "I've Wandered Many a Weary Mile" it is quickly restored in the succeeding stanza:

> Love is the main spring of existence—It
> Becomes a soul wherebye I live to love
> On all I see that dearest name is writ
> Falsehood is here—but truth has life above.

In fact, the movement of this section follows a clear pattern of descent and recovery. Temporary disillusionment occurs not only in the song mentioned, but also in the fifth, sixth, and seventh stanzas. At this point Clare leans more toward wrath than kindness in his attempt to comprehend his surroundings in the asylum and his reasons for being there. The extremity of his misgivings is most poignantly expressed in stanza seven where he even questions the validity of his love songs:

> How servile is the task to please alone
> Though beauty woo and love inspire the song.

As frequently happens in *Child Harold,* calm is restored suddenly, this time in the stanza referring to the comforting "forest queen." His recovery through four stanzas culminates in the final stanza of the section, a curious compound of satisfaction and regret, of nostalgia and implicit hope:

> I have had many loves—and seek no more—
> These solitudes my last delights shall be
> The leaf hid forest—and the lonely shore
> Seem to my mind like beings that are free
> Yet would I had some eye to smile on me
> Some heart where I could make a happy home in
> Sweet Susan that was wont my love to me
> And Bessey of the glen—for I've been roaming
> With both at morn and noon and dusky gloaming.

Progress from confidence through momentary uncertainty and back to a more complex, less didactic, type of assurance defines the movement of the section, but unity is maintained throughout by subordinating all moods to a general sense of possible, if not inevitable, improvement in his situation.

This section also establishes the major themes and preoccupations Clare is to explore. The necessity for truth, integrity, and love—the need for absolutes in the unstable world around him—continually surfaces in this section. Beginning with the truth of

poets and continuing through nature's eternal love, through love
as the "main spring of existence," to the central source of
absolute love in the poem, Mary, Clare stresses again and again
the desirability of concrete values on which to base human
relationships. Far more than the girl he knew in his youth, Mary
becomes his "ace of hearts, [his] muse of song / The pole star of
[his] being and decay." She is not only the object of his search
and inspiration for his song, but also the touchstone against which
all other elements of beauty, constancy, and love are measured.

She is also a central figure in a second complex of themes
which begins in this section. Clare explores several variations on
the theme of bondage and freedom, developing out of his
situation in the asylum a symbol of the mental, social, and literary
confinement which contrasts, generally, with the emotional
freedom he seeks through Mary. The first song, for example,
finds consolation in his natural surroundings even though he's "in
prison / Without any friends." The subdued optimism of this
entire section is neatly summarized in the second song, where he
stresses his paradoxical freedom in bondage:

> Though cares still will gather like clouds in my sky
> Though hopes may grow hopeless and fetters recoil
> While the sun of existance sheds light in my eye
> I'll be free in a prison and cling to the soil
> I'll cling to the spot where my first love was cherished
> Where my heart nay my soul unto Mary I gave
> And when my last hope and existance is perished
> Her memory will shine like a sun on my grave.

A plaintive note qualifies his dejection in the middle stanzas of
the section, especially in his already quoted realization of the
servility of writing love songs and in his sensation of decaying in
the asylum: "Now stagnant grows my too refined clay / I envy
birds their wings to flye away." He is physically confined in the
asylum but even more seriously he is, by his own definition, in
danger of losing his poetic integrity. If poets "must be truly
honest men / Tied to no mongrel laws on flatterys page," his
servility in composing the present poem in praise of Mary belies
his integrity. But the poem never does become an unqualified
panegyric on his past love; Mary is at times the subject of his
most ardent praise, but she is also one source of his misery—at
times, even, the embodiment of inconstancy:

>Nor night nor day nor sun nor shade
>Week month nor rolling year
>Repairs the breach wronged love hath made
>There madness—misery here
>Lifes lease was lengthened by her smiles
>—Are truth and love contrary
>No ray of hope my life beguiles
>I've lost love home and Mary.

Suitably, therefore, the section ends not with assurances of meeting Mary, but with a more general nostalgia for Susan and Bess, examples of general pastoral lovers.

Section Two, which includes the twelfth through the twentieth stanzas and three songs ("Written in a Thunder storm July 15th 1841," "O Mary Sing thy Songs to Me," and "Lovely Mary When We Parted"), opens with an abrupt, even violent, change of mood.[18] Nostalgia has given way to defiant bitterness:

>Cares gather round I snap their chains in two
>And smile in agony and laugh in tears
>Like playing with a deadly serpent—who
>Stings to the death.

The change is primarily one of tone rather than theme, though this stanza contemplates the same possibility of relief through death that preoccupied Clare in the previous section. But the new tone is reflected in a different imagery which substitutes for the natural images of enclosed chapel yards, sweet fern hills, and little "bridge with guiding rail" the paradoxes of smiling in agony and laughing in tears, not to mention the grotesquerie of playing with snakes. These new figures echo the madhouse imagery of stanzas five and six, interrelating the two sections but developing a momentary motif from one into the dominant imagery of the other. The remainder of the section moves from this frenetic posturing, through apathy, to a calm declaration of devotion to Mary.

Transition from frenzy to apathy is effectively achieved through the song that immediately succeeds the opening stanza of this section. "Written in a Thunder storm July 15th 1841" is consistent with the new mood of violence in the poem, but it utilizes violence to illustrate Clare's lack of energy and decaying mental powers. It reminds us of Lear on the heath, but perhaps more of Coleridge in his "Dejection: An Ode":

> The heavens are wrath—the thunders rattling peal
> Rolls like a vast volcano in the sky
> Yet nothing starts the apathy I feel
> Nor chills with fear eternal destiny
>
> My soul is apathy—a ruin vast
> Time cannot clear the ruined mass away
> My life is hell—the hopeless die is cast
> And manhoods prime is premature decay
>
> Roll on ye wrath of thunders—peal on peal
> Till worlds are ruins and myself alone
> Melt heart and soul cased in obdurate steel
> Till I can feel that nature is my throne
>
> I live in love sun of undying light
> And fathom my own heart for ways of good
> In its pure atmosphere day without night
> Smiles on the plains the forest and the flood
>
> Smile on ye elements of earth and sky
> Or frown in thunders as ye frown on me
> Bid earth and its delusions pass away
> But leave the mind as its creator free.

The violent storm is an effective measurement, through contrast, of the extent of his deadened emotions, of the apathy and listlessness which he begins to consider part of his "eternal destiny." The iron chain is an appropriate image secondary to the storm itself, indicating the severe bondage he feels here in contrast with the comforting restrictions of the forest in the previous section. The chains that he threatened to snap in the preceding stanza have become a case of "obdurate steel" cast from a hopeless die. The song itself is a passionate, therefore paradoxical, plea for the liberation of his imagination from apathy. He belies his apparent indifference with a spirited appeal to physical nature to break through the gloom he feels and restore the mental and emotional energy needed to experience his former intimacy with nature.

After the violence of the song Clare's mood subsides into the nightmare realm of apathy. The imagery remains surreal, depicting "gliding" serpents, "a frost bound thought that freezes

life to stone," and isolation on a *"lengthening* road" (my italics),
but the new tone gradually emerges out of the violence-apathy
dichotomy. The progress of his change is charted by the
apparently chronological movement which governs these stanzas
even though they were written in different manuscripts and at
different times. Stanza 13 refers to twilight as the setting for
Clare's musings on escape through death. Two stanzas later
twilight has turned to night and, later in the same stanza, to
midnight. Further movement is marked by the paradox at the
conclusion of stanza 16 where day provides not the usual relief
from the increasing darkness but confusion with night itself: "day
seems my night and night seems blackest hell." This intensification of darkness corresponds with Clare's deepening sense of
estrangement from nature. With the word "hell" marking the
extremity of his separation, the section begins to turn toward a
renewed sensitivity. The moment of change, in stanza 17, is
marked by his first mention of Mary in this series of stanzas. His
memory of her power to overcome previous periods of
depression leads to a momentary recovery here. Retreat into the
past partially compensates for his loss of intimacy with nature
and reaffirms his faith in Mary. His recovery is reflected in the
final stanza of the section. Even though the ice imagery partakes
of the same nightmare quality as the rest of the imagery in the
section, the tone is quite different from that of earlier stanzas:

> I loved her in all climes beneath the sun
> Her name was like a jewel in my heart
> Twas heavens own choice—and so Gods will be done
> Love ties that keep unbroken cannot part
> Nor can cold abscence sever or desert
> That simple beauty blessed with matchless charms
> Oceans have rolled between us—not to part
> E'en Icelands snows true loves delirium warms
> For there Ive dreamed—and Mary filled my arms.

The final impression is of Clare's extreme sensitivity. His
regained composure dominates the simple melody of his
poignant appeal to Mary in the first of the two concluding songs:

> O Mary sing thy songs to me
> Of love and beautys melody

> My sorrows sink beneath distress
> My deepest griefs are sorrowless
> So used to glooms and cares am I
> My fearless troubles seem as joy
> O Mary sing thy songs to me
> Of love and beautys melody.

This is only the first stanza, but it illustrates Clare's altered mood. His recovery produces not the violent alternative to apathy that he had demanded at the outset, but a plaintive admission that he is still capable of subtle emotion, that he still responds poetically to his present situation. A similar tone modified by a greater confidence in the future informs the final song in the section, "Lovely Mary When We Parted." Clare is lonely, but devoted; having lost his indifference, he has replaced it with a related but less indolent feeling of loss and isolation. The final stanza of the song offers a fitting conclusion to this alteration. His retreat into the past, at the crucial turning point of the section, culminates in a newfound hope and a confidence in his spiritual if not physical relationship with Mary:

> And by that hope that lingers last
> For heaven when lifes hell is past
> By time the present—past and gone
> I've loved thee—and I love thee on
> Thy beauty made youths life divine
> Till my soul grew a part of thine
> Mary I mourn no pleasures gone—
> The past has made us both as one.

From the extremes of apathy and violence Clare has moved through a session of self-examination to an awakened sensitivity arising out of his contemplation of Mary. His progress through the whole poem is implicit in the contrast between the ending of these first two sections, the first losing itself in nostalgia for typical pastoral girls, and the second finding personal identity in a union with his ideal of womanhood in the specific form of Mary Joyce.

In Section Three Clare extracts out of the autumn landscape a corollary for his own mellow state of mind. No longer apathetic, he writes (in stanzas 21 to 28 and the four interspersed songs)

with a calm assurance that nature and his memory of Mary still
actively compensate for his present bleak prospects.[19] The
contrast with previous sections is apparent in the calm tone and
return to natural imagery in the opening stanza:

> Now melancholly autumn comes anew
> With showery clouds and fields of wheat tanned brown
> Along the meadow banks I peace pursue
> And see the wild flowers gleaming up and down
> Like sun and light—the ragworts golden crown
> Mirrors like sunshine when sunbeams retire
> And silver yarrow—there's the little town
> And oer the meadows gleams that slender spire
> Reminding me of one—and waking fond desire.

Again Clare captures the mood of an entire section in a short,
evocative phrase. The gently paradoxical "fond desire" describes his tone, not passionate or indifferent as before, but
tempering the urgency of desire with the tranquility of a love
long restrained and eventually refined into peaceful affection.

This tone of restraint is also evident in the precise control he
exercises over two, in particular, of the songs in this section. The
more evocative of them has a hymn-like quality which not only
contributes to the tone, but also conveys Clare's patient, but
mildly anxious and wistful, biding of time until he meets Mary
again:

> Sweet days while God your blessings send
> I call your joys my own
> —And if I have an only friend
> I am not left alone
>
> She sees the fields the trees the spires
> Which I can daily see
> And if true love her heart inspires
> Life still has joys for me
>
> She sees the wild flower in the dells
> That in my rambles shine
> The sky that oer her homestead dwells
> Looks sunny over mine

The cloud that passes where she dwells
In less than half an hour
Darkens around these orchard dells
Or melts a sudden shower

The wind that leaves the sunny south
And fans the orchard tree
Might steal the kisses from her mouth
And waft her voice to me

O when will autumn bring the news
Now harvest browns the fen
That Mary as my vagrant muse
And I shall meet agen.

Clare's delicate response to the elements of nature emphasizes the tenderness of his feeling for Mary. Their union is completed by their being embraced by a natural order which touches both of them, physically as well as imaginatively.[20] This union-in-separation is another of the controlling paradoxes in the poem; the song is a lyrical elaboration on the theme mentioned in the last line of Section Two "The past has made us both as one" and the final line of the stanza immediately preceding the song: "Our lives are two—our end and aim is one."

The pathos of the second song arises from this same apparent contradiction. In "No Single Hour Can Stand for Nought" Clare diverts his observation from the external evidence of his proximity to Mary to his own intuitive sense of loss. In spite of his affection she continues remote in space, as he has realized in "Sweet Days While God Your Blessings Send," and in time, as he notices here:

No single hour can stand for nought
No moment hand can move
But calenders a aching thought
Of my first lonely love.

The four verses that follow this opening one examine the source of his "aching thought" in the suppression of first love. But he closes the song with a final assertion of his faith in Mary's

constant influence on him even when he cannot praise her out
loud:

> When words refuse before the crowd
> My Marys name to give
> The muse in silence sings aloud
> And there my love will live.

The somber tone of his musings here is consistent with the type
of pleasures he associates with autumn in the descriptive stanzas
that complement the songs. Except for the incomprehensible
twenty-third stanza which seems never to have been properly
revised, the pattern these stanzas follow is one of healthy
appreciation of nature at the beginning and end, with a brief
two-stanza introspection in between. This introspection marks a
temporary moment of equilibrium in which Clare achieves a
measure of self-knowledge and contentment. Referring to the
pleasures of fame, peace, hope, and love that he has mentioned
in the previous stanza, he assesses their impact on his life in
stanza 27:

> Though they are blazoned in the poets song
> As all the comforts which our lifes contain
> I read and sought such joys my whole life long
> And found the best of poets sung in vain
> But still I read and sighed and sued again.
> And lost no purpose where I had the will
> I almost worshiped when my toils grew vain
> Finding no antidote my pains to kill
> I sigh a poet and a lover still.

Finding none of these pleasures enduring, he has sought and
found consolation in writing love poetry. The three succeeding
songs are evidence of his remaining powers as a poet and lover
and are dominated by the wistfulness of that sigh. But he
concludes the section with a return to the more positive pleasure
evoked by the autumn landscape:

> Now harvest smiles embrowning all the plain
> The sun of heaven oer its ripeness shines
> 'Peace-plenty' has been sung nor sung in vain
> As all bring forth the makers grand designs

> —Like gold that brightens in some hidden mines
> His nature is the wealth that brings increase
> To all the world—his sun forever shines
> —He hides his face and troubles they increase
> He smiles—the sun looks out in wealth and peace.

This attitude is quickly reversed in the short Fourth Section, where Clare submits to bitterness and despair. This movement, comprised of five stanzas and three songs, approaches his *Don Juan* in its pervasive tone of recrimination:[21]

> This life is made of lying and grimace
> This world is filled with whoring and decieving
> Hypocrisy ne'er masks an honest face
> Story's are told—but seeing is believing.

The absolutes he sought in the early stanzas—truth and honesty, love and constancy—are contradicted by his present experience. The reason for his disillusionment is not hard to find. In one of these songs he comments that Mary is "abscent every where." It is more than coincidence that her absence is the central feature of the songs while the lack of truth dominates his introspection in the stanzas. The extent of his despondency can be felt when he attempts, in stanzas 30 and 31, to retreat again into the past. He ruminates on the pleasant images of his childhood, trying to recapture his former responses to them. This time the result is only a deepened despair: "Yet still the picture turns my bosom chill / And leaves a void—nor love nor hope may fill." Even his attempt in stanza 33 to argue himself out of this state of mind by appealing to Mary's ability to "cheer [him] when the storm is bye" is belied by the song that follows it. That song concludes with his first admission that Mary's absence might be permanent:

> I seek her in the early morn
> But cannot meet her face again
> Sweet Mary she is abscent still
> And much I fear she ever will.

Clare stresses the separation element of the unity-in-separation paradox throughout this section. In this song, and more concisely in "Did I Know Where to Meet Thee," he switches the emphasis from one side of that dichotomy to the other. No longer

contemplating her faithfulness in spite of long absence, he now
stresses her emotional distance from him in spite of her physical
proximity: "Though Mary live's near me—she seems far away."

The climax of *Child Harold* occurs, appropriately, in the
central movement. Stretching from stanza 34 to 41 and including
three songs, Section Five forms not only the structural center of
the poem, but also the unmistakable high point of Clare's
emotional odyssey, his only moment of pure joy.[22] The arrangement of this section produces a correlative emotional experience
in the reader. Clare leads us through a sequence of descriptive
passages—all emphasizing his recovery from the disillusionment
of the previous section—which rises toward the end like a
symphonic crescendo to an expression of ecstasy before falling
away slightly to a concluding emotional plateau.

A tone of normality is established from the beginning. Clare
concentrates on the fullness of autumn before the harvest,
finding in it a rustic healthiness that reflects his own response to
nature:

> The autumn morn looks mellow as the fruit
> And ripe as harvest—every field and farm
> Is full of health and toil—yet never mute
> With rustic mirth and peace the day is warm
> The village maid with gleans upon her arm
> Brown as the hazel nut from field to field
> Goes cheerily—the valleys native charm—
> I seek for charms that autumn best can yield
> In mellowing wood and time ybleaching field.

Turning from external description to a subjective response to the
landscape, the song following this passage supports the new tone
by expressing the fullness of heart Clare feels toward Mary. The
ripe grain and mellow wood imply imminent change, but Clare
feels confident of the permanence of his love for her:

> The fading woods the russet grange
> The hues of nature may desert
> But nought in me shall find a change
> To wrong the angel of my heart.

He pledges a constancy that requires only his memory of their early relationship, not her physical presence as in the previous section, to maintain itself:

> Her name my lonely quiet cheers
> And cheer it will what e'er may be
> While Mary lives to think of me.

Succeeding stanzas continue Clare's enjoyment of autumn, slowly increasing his pleasure and sense of well-being. Mist dominates the first of these stanzas, curling "thick and grey / As cottage smoke" and condensing on the seeded grass "beaded with pearls of dew at early day." Thereafter the sun vanquishes the mist and transforms the landscape into a source of more intense pleasure:

> What mellowness these harvest days unfold
> In the strong glances of the midday sun
> The homesteads very grass seems changed to gold
> The light in golden shadows seems to run
> And tinges every spray it rests upon
> With that rich harvest hue of sunny joy
> Nature lifes sweet companion cheers alone—
> The hare starts up before the shepherd boy
> And partridge coveys wir on russet wings of joy.

The landscape, we soon learn, is enhanced by the creatures that share Clare's place in it as well as by his memory of childhood experiences in the same location and the church bells that unite his past with his present pleasure: "Aye nothing seems so happy and sublime / As sabbath bells and their delightfull chime." But what contributes most to his quiet enjoyment here is the solitude that enables him to feel a sense of reciprocal communion with nature, and allows his unrestricted imagination to revel in the stimuli provided by the sights and sounds around him. With solitude, the "partner of [his] life," the "autumn air / Mellows [his] heart to harmony." This harmony gradually encompasses the village bells which Clare repeatedly notices in these stanzas until they reveal the true source of his joy:

> For in that hamlet lives my rising sun
> Whose beams hath cheered me all my lorn life long

My heart to nature there was early won
For she was natures self—and still my song
Is her through sun and shade through right and wrong
On her my memory forever dwells
The flower of Eden—evergreen of song
Truth in my heart the same love story tells
—I love the music of those village bells.

The culmination of Clare's emotional experience occurs while he
stands exposed on the fens looking across the meadow to Mary's
village and listening to the bells from Glinton church. For the
moment he is supremely happy and confident. Mary is united in
his mind with nature, "for she was natures self," and the truth he
has sought throughout the poem has been confirmed: "Truth in
my heart the same love story tells." He bursts into unrestrained
song.

The toast to Mary marks the moment of purest exhilaration in
the poem. In it he abandons himself to a cavalier outburst of
instinctive joy:

Heres a health unto thee bonnie lassie O
Leave the thorns o' care wi' me
And whatever I may be
Here's happiness to thee
Bonny lassie O.

There are three other verses to the song, each repeating the
same theme with minor variations. Outside the poem this would
be a pretty ordinary, though competent, imitation of a traditional
folksong, but within its context it gives us a precise indication of
the poet's state of mind at this point, an indication of his
emotional violation of the firm control he has striven to maintain
in the rest of the poem. In fact, the derivative nature of the
song—it is the least original and personal in *Child Harold*—
contributes to our understanding of Clare's ecstasy. The words
are not as important as their dramatic context; the mere act of
singing illustrates the purity of his emotion at this time. The
nature of the song indicates the depths of his roots in the folk
tradition; in moments of intense feeling he reaches for a
traditional form for his effusions. Because thought, imagery, and
subtlety of sensation are alien to the moment, their absence

reinforces the impact of his song. Clare is experiencing pure joy, uncomplicated by rational assessment of his predicament. That we can see the fragility of his ecstasy—the thorns are there, even though he is confident he can bear them—only adds an ironic touch of pathos.

The song gives way to a single stanza celebrating the unity of all creatures within nature, followed immediately by a song which reintroduces Clare's former doubts. "Her Cheeks Are Like Roses" is a song of dedication, but in contrast to the unrestrained joy of the previous song, it embodies a conditional aspect to his love: "And her beauty is mine / *If* her heart it is true" (italics mine). Clare's future depends on forces outside his control. "If theres truth in her bosom," he says, "I shall see her again." The song is still an expression of confidence, but it is more restrained than the previous one; it marks a partial retreat from his unalloyed pleasure, a realization of the uncertainty of forces outside his own unquestioned constancy.

The subject of truth is picked up again in the three stanzas that comprise the fragmentary Section Six.[23] But now truth and its corollary, love, are embattled, though never quite overcome, by what Clare calls, without clarification, "evil lies." In an image that Blake might have used he describes the organic nature of this conflict:

> —So lies keep climbing round loves sacred stem
> Blighting fair truth whose leaf is evergreen
> Whose roots are the hearts fibres and whose sun
> The soul that cheers and smiles it into bloom
> Till heaven proclaims that truth can never die.

The imagery in this section is primarily figurative, supporting a plethora of abstractions rather than developing into literal images directly from Clare's response to his natural surroundings. Unfortunately, Clare's statement is not immediately explicable, although his mood reveals something of the trauma resulting from the passing of his recent epiphany triggered by the village bells. Clare's violent indignation at the nebulous forces which destroyed that experience is evoked through the imagery, though not this time the actual description, of a thunderstorm:

> The lightenings vivid flashes—rend the cloud
> That rides like castled crags along the sky
> And splinters them to fragments—while aloud
> The thunders heavens artillery vollies bye
> Trees crash, earth trembles—beast[s] prepare to flye
> Almighty what a crash—yet man is free
> And walks unhurt while danger seems so nigh—
> Heavens archway now the rainbow seems to be
> That spans the eternal round of earth and sky and sea.

This storm is another example of Clare's habit of referring back to earlier themes, motifs, and images. And it demonstrates his progress. Whereas he formerly invoked the violence in nature to pierce his apathy, he now uses it to emphasize his almost frenetic belief in the indestructibility of hope. This mood ceases as abruptly as it began, however, and in the next section a more subdued Clare emerges from the emotional turbulence found in this and the previous section.

This next group of stanzas and songs is more satisfying both for the mood it conveys and for its form.[24] It opens with stanza 45, a return to the tranquility and composure of autumnal nature which reflects a less ecstatic state of mind in Clare, not joy this time but the happiness of resignation: "For natures every place is still resigned / To happiness—new life's in every view." Nature, like Clare, has passed its zenith, reaching a peacefulness that contains reminders of what has passed:

> The lake that held a mirror to the sun
> Now curves with wrinkles in the stillest place
> The autumn wind sounds hollow as a gun
> And water stands in every swampy place
> Yet in these fens peace harmony and grace
> The attributes of nature are alied
> The barge with naked mast in sheltered place
> Beside the brig close to the bank is tied
> While small waves plashes by its bulky side.

What was once a mirror is now wrinkled, the wind is hollow, and the mast naked, but the scene maintains its charm just as Clare continues to respond no matter how altered from his previous abandonment in joy. In his present mood he sings one of his most effective songs, one that draws upon the character of its setting to illustrate the complex mood he feels:

> The floods come oer the meadow leas
> The dykes are full and brimming
> Field furrows reach the horses knees
> Where wild ducks oft are swimming
> The skyes are black the fields are bare
> The trees their coats are loosing
> The leaves are dancing in the air
> The sun its warmth refusing.

The repletion of the landscape seems at first to reflect the fullness of the viewer's heart, even though it is qualified by the bleak sky and fields and the reluctant sun. The description of the sun is particularly appropriate because the mere reference to it reminds us of its earlier predominance in scenes of delight, especially its mellowing powers in stanza 36. Here, though, Clare's feeling that it withholds its warmth indicates the extent of his despondency. Not until the end of the second verse, however, do we learn that the scene is inadequate to illustrate the full extent of his mood:

> Brown are the flags and fadeing sedge
> And tanned the meadow plains
> Bright yellow is the osier hedge
> Beside the brimming drains
> The crows sit on the willow tree
> The lake is full below
> But still the dullest thing I see
> Is self that wanders slow.

He elaborates on his state of mind in the final stanza:

> The dullest scenes are not so dull
> As thoughts I cannot tell
> The brimming dykes are not so full
> As my hearts silent swell
> I leave my troubles to the winds
> With none to share a part
> The only joy my feeling finds
> Hides in an aching heart.

Clare's melancholy rises above the clichés of the eighteenth-century School of Melancholy. He has found the appropriate vehicle for expressing his precise mood, a mood of overwhelming

heartache which remains with him after the two violent
extremes of passion in the preceding sections have passed.

He is not so fortunate in his attempt to explain his situation
rationally in the stanza that follows this song. His reliance on
gothic similes like "ruined cities" and death-like crowds fails to
enhance the personal emotion in his final couplet:

> The strongest bitterest thing that life can prove
> Is womans undisguise of hate and love.

From a resigned happiness to this temporary bitterness has been
a short step, but he recovers his equilibrium in a subsequent
group of songs which are based on variations of the method and
theme in "The Floods Come Oer the Meadow Leas." In "I Think
of Thee at Early Day," for example, the season has progressed to
the brink of winter but Clare's heart reflects no change:

> I can't expect to meet thee now
> The winter floods begin
> The wind sighs throu the naked bough
> Sad as my heart within.

The isolated stanza between this song and the next heralds the
arrival of winter—"Tis winter and the fields are bare and
waste"—and Clare finds a measure of consolation in that season:

> Bare fields the frozen lake and leafless grove
> Are natures grand religion and true love.

The next song, however, gives a different nuance to Clare's
somber attitude. It is a quiet expression of Mary's value to him,
without any remarkable departure from other songs of devotion
to her except its subdued tone. The final song in the section,
though, reaffirms Clare's resignation:

> In this cold world without a home
> Disconsolate I go
> The summer looks as cold to me
> As winters frost and snow
> Though winters scenes are dull and drear

A colder lot I prove
No home had I through all the year
But Marys honest love.

From that beginning Clare wends his way through effective
statements of loss which are heightened by his use of the past
tense when referring to Mary. The song ends with a less
complicated sense of dejection than the section began with:

But now loves hopes are all bereft
A lonely man I roam
And absent Mary long hath left
My heart without a home.

Gone is the hope and expectation of earlier songs; Clare is
slowly, painfully coming down from his emotional peak.

The descent continues in Section Eight. We cannot be sure
how Clare would have organized the poem from this point on
because the remaining stanzas and songs follow his order in the
High Beech notebook, from which he copied and rearranged
most of the earlier part of the poem into his fair-copy book.
Fortunately, the stanzas which are not physically rearranged
have been numbered, presumably to indicate the order Clare
intended for them. Only two of the stanzas bear a number which
contradicts their position in the sequence. The first appears as
the forty-ninth stanza in Robinson and Summerfield's edition but
bears the number 27, implying it belongs elsewhere. Since it fits
both the subject and the tone of Section Eight, however, we will
deal with it, cautiously, as stanza 49. On the other hand, the fifty-
first stanza bears the number 18 and seems to fit better, because
of its subject, in the proximity of the later stanza bearing the
same number (i.e., stanza 66).

The final twenty-eight stanzas seem to fall naturally into two
segments, a brief expression of complete despair and a longer
discussion of the nature of love. The shorter section, Section
Eight, includes the forty-ninth through the fifty-fourth stanzas,
with the possible exception of number 51.[25] The central stanza of
the five forms a pivot for the section, since the first half reflects
Clare's appreciation of spring while the second half sinks into
dejection at his lost capacity to respond to it:

Now Come The Balm And Breezes Of The Spring
Not With The Pleasure's Of My Early Day's
When Nature Seemed One Endless Song To Sing
A Joyous Melody And Happy Praise
Ah Would They Come Agen—But Life Betrays
Quicksands and Gulphs And Storms That Howl and Sting
All Quiet Into Madness And Delays
Care Hides The Sunshine With Its Raven Wing
And Hell Glooms Sadness Oer The Songs Of Spring.

He concludes the section by picturing "Wastes Without Springs
And Homes Without A Friend." Significantly, there are no songs
in this section; the lyrical impulse is incompatible with this vision
of his present circumstances.

But the final section begins with a song. "Say What is Love"
combines several themes from earlier parts of the poem, notably
those of freedom in bondage, the inconstancy of love, and Mary
as the focal point of whatever ideal love Clare can still
comprehend.[26] But it also poses, in its title, the central question
to be explained in this final section. The remainder of the poem,
despite its frequent tendencies to digress, continually returns to
discuss the ramifications of this question. The four stanzas
immediately following the song examine the misery of a loveless
existence as exemplified by an orphan "On Whose Young Face A
Mother Never Smiled." For the first time in the poem we meet a
less self-indulgent Clare, capable of and willing to move outside
himself and consider his own problems in the context of other
sufferers. The effect is a reassurance for him that the orphan's
lot is not beyond hope: "Providence That Grand Eternal
Calm / Is With Him Like The Sunshine In The Sky." In the next
four stanzas he explores an opposing variation on the experience
of love, the ideal pastoral love. Here he integrates the life of
rural maids with his own youth and discovers not reassurance this
time but a similar tempering of the ideal, both in his own and in
the general rural experience:

Sweet Bessey Maid Of Health And Fancys Pure
How Did I Woo Thee Once—Still Unforgot
But Promises In Love Are Never Sure.

This final section reveals an enquiring, almost objective,

certainly a more mature, mind. The resulting tone is relatively
balanced: inquisitive but knowledgeable, sorrowful but consoled,
resigned but occasionally defiant. It encompasses a song to his
wife, the only woman who remained faithful to him, which acts
as a counterpoint to another song to Mary. The final song of the
whole poem mentions neither woman, but is a fitting conclusion
to the sequence of lyrical moments embodied in the *Child
Harold* songs. Its universality as well as its direct simplicity and
genuine emotion are reminiscent of Wordsworth's Lucy poems:

> I saw her in my springs young choice
> Ere loves hopes looked upon the crowd
> Ere loves first secrets found a voice
> Or dared to speak the name aloud
>
> I saw her in my boyish hours
> A Girl as fair as heaven above
> When all the world seemed strewn with flowers
> And every pulse and look was love
>
> I saw her when her heart was young
> I saw her when my heart was true
> When truth was all the themes I sung
> And Love the only muse I knew
>
> Ere infancy had left her brow
> I seemed to love her from her birth
> And thought her then as I do now
> The dearest angel upon earth.

Balancing this pure lyricism we find Clare's continuing self-
assessment which has characterized most of the *Child Harold*
stanzas:

> Flow on my verse though barren thou mayest be
> Of thought—Yet sing and let thy fancys roll
> In Early days thou sweept a mighty sea
> All calm in troublous deeps and spurned controul
> Thou fire and iceberg to an aching soul
> And still an angel in my gloomy way
> Far better opiate then the draining bowl
> Still sing my muse to drive cares fiends away
> Nor heed what loitering listener hears the lay.

Something of Clare's achievement is indicated by this belated invocation. While his verse has not been entirely "barren of thought,' the intellectual content has been subordinated throughout to the lyrical and the emotional. Even the extremes he here suggests through fire and ice pervade *Child Harold*, which itself has traced just the sort of emotional release he mentions in the concluding lines.

The poem ends without a logical summary or final statement of theme, but with a stanza designed to leave us on Clare's emotional plateau, not as optimistic as we started out, but not as despondent as at times in the course of the journey. It forms the culmination of the group of stanzas discussed earlier in this chapter which return to the forest image. It distracts us rather than concludes the themes Clare has explored, leaving us with an appropriate conflict between the song of birds—always Clare's measurement of joy—and the splendid but unsatisfactory palace of love in an urban environment:

> Sweet is the song of Birds for that restores
> The soul to harmony the mind to love
> Tis natures song of freedom out of doors
> Forests beneath free winds and clouds above
> The Thrush and Nightingale and timid dove
> Breathe music round me where the gipseys dwell—
> Pierced hearts left burning in the doubts of love
> Are desolate where crowds and citys dwell—
> The splendid palace seems the gates of hell.

The poem's organization has followed a pattern of varying moods; it is suitable that we should be left with an evocation of contrasting moods rather than a literal concluding statement.

Unlike other Romantic poems of self-assessment which tend to derive a comprehensive world view from the process of personal reexamination, Clare's poem juxtaposes, throughout, a series of temporary answers to persistent questions. The result is not a confident metaphysic but an attempt to reduce a multiplicity of contradictory facts and emotions to at least an ontological paradox. The paradox remains inexplicable in a rational way, but derives some intellectual insight from apparently opposing observations. In place of the certainty reflected in the form of Blake's, or Wordsworth's, or Coleridge's poetry, Clare can offer only an unflinching exposure of the problem. In some ways *Child*

Harold's diffuseness, tempered though it is by the formal devices already mentioned, is more convincing than the confidence underlying Blake's tendency to reduce answers to epigrammatic conciseness, or Wordsworth's earnest self-confidence, or Coleridge's conversational pontification. No other of Clare's poems, perhaps no other Romantic poem, gives such an intricate revelation of man trying to justify the apparent conflict between his subjective response to, and rational assessment of, human existence. In this respect Clare is closer to Arnold searching for certainty amidst ignorant armies that clash by night, or to Hardy trying to reconcile the thrush's song with the context in which it is sung.

CHAPTER 7

Conclusion

BECAUSE Clare's theory of poetic composition stressed the value of symbols elicited from nature, we might expect to find a large number of them in his work. And since these symbols are the result of a single mind responding to its environment over half a century, we might be justified in looking for a unified pattern which would reflect the changing nature of these responses as the mind itself matured. In practice Clare's poetry returns again and again to the same group of metaphors and symbols; as a consequence, we can measure his growth, both personally and poetically, in his altering attitude to them. His recurring motifs include the "book" of nature and the bird as a symbol of poetic utterance, as well as the sun and wind which dominate so much of his verse. A more pervasive pattern of interrelated symbols which gives a sense of profound unity to the body of his work has been noted by Eric Robinson and Geoffrey Summerfield:

In the landscape of Eden before the Fall, Clare's boyhood love, Mary Joyce, is present—she is the Eve to Clare's Adam. Unless we recognize that this is the conscious pattern of imagery in Clare's poetry, we are bound to miss a great deal of his point. Everything in his boyhood environment assumes a new character, a vividness far beyond accurate natural history, a deeper identity because it is part of what Clare calls "Loves register." In this "register," not just trees but every single tree, not just grass but every single blade of grass is a special act of the Creator and participates in the freshness before the Fall.[1]

In this scheme Eden symbolizes not only childhood innocence but a complex state of mind which, although primarily experienced in childhood, could also recur in select, but brief, periods throughout the rest of his life. The decreasing ability to maintain this state as he grew older, therefore, represented for him the loss of Eden, and the mental state that resulted from this loss he expressed in another symbol, the wasteland.

The bulk of his mature work is concerned with this wasteland and with momentary glimpses of Eden which were in fact revivals of the state of mind he associated with the bliss of his early life. The loss was reflected historically by the post-enclosure landscape in which the garden became a wasteland, cursed by toil as Adam and Eve were:

> I hate the plough that comes to dissaray
> Her holiday delights—and labours toil
> Seems vulgar curses on the sunny soil
> And man the only object that distrains
> Earths garden into deserts for his gains.[2]

But in other poems the wasteland is less literal, more symbolic of Clare's own, inner, turmoil:

> . . . Life Betrays
> Quicksands and Gulphs And Storms That Howl And Sting
> All Quiet Into Madness And Delays
> Care Hides The Sunshine With Its Raven Wing
> And Hell Glooms Sadness Oer The Songs Of Spring
> Like Satans Warcry First In Paradise
> When Love Lay Sleeping On The Flowery Slope.[3]

During that part of his life which he compared to a wasteland, however, he never lost sight of the possibility of moments of edenic insight recurring. Even in his desert we get glimpses of paradise which make his life outside Eden tolerable and at times even enjoyable. He formulated no theory, either psychological or philosophical, to support his view, but he was constantly aware of the effect of these glimpses on his state of mind:

> The healthfull mind that muses and inhales
> The green eyed dews of morning finds his way
> To paradise Gods choice self planted vales.[4]

A similar concept is stated in "Sighing for Retirement," with the addition of the wasteland-Eden dichotomy:

> To common eyes they only seem
> A desert waste and drear;
> To taste and love they always shine,
> A garden through the year.[5]

Taste and love combine to transform nature into a paradise, a process he describes more precisely in "Shadows of Taste":

> Minds spring as various as the leaves of trees
> To follow taste and all her sweets explore
> And Edens make where deserts spread before.[6]

His conversion of the desert into an Eden produced brief periods of intense response to the beauties of nature which provided the germ for many of his mature poems. The existence of these glimpses was enough to sustain him in the wasteland of his later life. Although the details differ from those of Wordsworth's "spots of time," their essential character and certainly their effect was similar. Clare's experience taught him, too, that

> Invigorating thoughts from former years,
> Might fix the wavering balance of my mind,
> And haply meet reproaches, too, whose power
> May spur me on, in manhood now mature,
> To honorable toil.[7]

As symbols, Eden and the desert provide additional structure to the body of Clare's work by marking a constant polarity between moods of sensitivity, freedom, and love, and those of melancholy, anger, and despair. They also demonstrate development by tracing the gradual decline of edenic experiences into the predominantly barren landscape of his later years.

Clare's ability to conceive symbols larger than those of a single poem and to apply them more or less consistently throughout his life is another indication of his true stature as a poet. He is gradually gaining the recognition he deserves and the amount of his available writings is slowly increasing. He appears with more frequent and extensive representation in modern anthologies of the Romantic Period and is rescued from the backwater of "minor poetry" in the *New Cambridge Bibliography of English Literature.* From the evidence, it appears his reputation grows according to the formula he himself approved: "the quiet progress of a name gaining its ground by gentle degrees in the world's esteem is the best living shadow of fame to follow."[8]

Notes and References

Where two sources are given for one poem, the first cited is the one quoted. The second is a less reliable but more easily accessible source. Manuscripts prefixed by a letter (e.g., MS A54) are from the collection at the Peterborough Museum and those with only a number (e.g., MS 20) are from the Northampton Public Library. The number following the manuscript number is the page number. If a quoted passage is not noted it belongs to the poem noted immediately before it, unless otherwise stated in the text.

Chapter One

1. *Sketches in the Life of John Clare Written by Himself,* ed. Edmund Blunden (London: Cobden-Sanderson, 1931), p. 45. Hereafter cited as *Sketches.*
2. *Sketches,* p. 47.
3. *The Prose of John Clare,* eds. J. W. and Anne Tibble (London: Routledge and Kegan Paul, 1951), pp. 18–19. Herafter cited as *Prose.*
4. *Sketches,* p. 59.
5. *Prose,* p. 34.
6. *The Letters of John Clare,* eds. J. W. and Anne Tibble (London: Routledge and Kegan Paul, 1951), p. 102. Hereafter cited as *Letters.*
7. *Sketches,* p. 87.
8. *Letters,* p. 123.
9. Ibid., p. 294.
10. Ibid., p. 293.
11. *Sketches,* p. 72.
12. *The Prose Works of Thomas Hood* (Philadelphia: Porter and Coates, n.d.), vol. 1, pp. 104–5.
13. *Letters,* p. 196.
14. John Barrell, *The Idea of Landscape and the Sense of Place 1730–1840* (Cambridge: Cambridge University Press, 1972), p. 176.
15. J. W. and Anne Tibble, *John Clare: A Life,* rev. ed. (London: Michael Joseph, 1972), p. 307.
16. *John Clare: A Life,* p. 310.

17. Quoted from *Clare: The Critical Heritage,* ed. Mark Storey (London: Routledge and Kegan Paul, 1973), pp. 242-3.

18. Cyrus Redding, *Past Celebrities I Have Known* (London: Charles J. Skeet, 1866), vol. 2, pp. 133-5.

19. *Letters,* p. 253.

Chapter Two

1. John Middleton Murry, *John Clare and Other Studies* (London: Peter Nevill, 1950), p. 8. Hereafter cited as Murry.

2. John Speirs, "Review of *Poems of John Clare,*" *Scrutiny,* 4 (1935), 86.

3. Murry, p. 8.

4. Ibid., p. 21.

5. *Prose,* p. 227.

6. Ibid., p. 53.

7. Ibid., p. 142.

8. Ibid., p. 175.

9. Ibid., p. 118.

10. Cyrus Redding, "Clare the Poet," *English Journal,* 20 (1841), 308-9.

11. Harold Bloom, *The Visionary Company* (Garden City, N.Y.: Doubleday, 1961), passim.

12. *Selected Poems of John Clare,* ed. Geoffrey Grigson (London: Routledge and Kegan Paul, 1950), p. 16.

13. Mark Storey, *The Poetry of John Clare* (London: Macmillan, 1974), p. 146. Hereafter cited as Storey.

14. *The Poems of John Clare,* ed. J. W. Tibble (London: Dent, 1935), vol. 2, pp. 383-4. Hereafter cited as *Poems.*

15. *Prose,* p. 223.

16. Ibid., p. 211.

17. *Selected Poems and Prose of John Clare,* eds. Eric Robinson and Geoffrey Summerfield (London: Oxford University Press, 1967), pp. 112-16. Hereafter cited as *Selected Poems.*

18. *Prose,* p. 257.

19. "Pastoral Poesy," MS A54-269. *Poems,* vol. 2, pp. 49-50.

20. *Poems,* vol. 1, p. viii.

21. M. H. Abrams, *The Mirror and the Lamp* (New York: Norton, 1958), p. 35.

22. *Prose,* p. 176.

23. "Sand Martin," *Selected Poems,* p. 69; "The Snowdrop," MS A5-33, *Poems,* vol. 1, p. 129.

24. "A Woodland Seat III," MS A54-375; *Poems,* vol. 2, p. 143.

25. *Prose,* p. 174.

26. Ralph Cohen, "David Hume's Experimental Method and the

Theory of Taste," *Journal of English Literary History*, 25 (1958), 272.

27. R. L. Brett, "The Aesthetic Sense and Taste in the Literary Criticism of the Early Eighteenth Century," *Review of English Studies*, 20 (1944), 207.

28. Brett, *Review of English Studies*, 20 (1944), 207.

29. MS B2-271a; *Poems*, vol. 1, p. 279.

30. MS A54-422; *Poems*, vol. 2, p. 327.

31. MS A42-125; *Prose*, p. 228.

32. "Pastoral Poesy," MS A54-269; *Poems*, vol. 2, pp. 49-50.

33. This term is also used in "Dawning of Genius" where taste "endears" the joy a sensitive shepherd feels in his native environment.

34. *Selected Poems*, pp. 112-16.

35. "A Woodland Seat III," MS A54-375; *Poems*, vol. 2, p. 143.

36. *The Later Poems of John Clare*, eds. Eric Robinson and Geoffrey Summerfield (Manchester: The University Press, 1964), p. 146. Hereafter cited as *Later Poems*.

37. *Selected Poems*, pp. 112-16.

38. "The Moorehens Nest," *Selected Poems*, pp. 79-82.

39. *Selected Poems*, pp. 112-16.

40. MS A5-10; *Poems*, vol. 1, pp. 69-70.

41. "Universal Goodness," MS A54-420; *Poems*, vol. 2, p. 308.

42. *Selected Poems*, pp. 69-72.

43. "On Visiting a Favourite Place," MS A54-254; *Poems*, vol. 2, pp. 259-61.

44. "Sighing for Retirement," *The Poems of John Clare's Madness*, ed. Geoffrey Grigson (London: Routledge and Kegan Paul, 1949), p. 57. Hereafter cited as *Poems of Madness*.

45. "The Voice of Nature," MS A51-106; *Poems*, vol. 2, pp. 39-40.

46. MS 3-164; *Poems*, vol. 1, p. 276.

47. MS 3-167; *Poems*, vol. 1, p. 133.

48. MS 4-49; *Poems*, vol. 1, p. 237.

49. MS A57-13; *Poems*, vol. 2, p. 304.

50. MS A54-269; *Poems*, vol. 2, pp. 49-50.

51. MS 4-38; *Poems*, vol. 1, pp. 69-70.

52. "Pastoral Poesy," MS A54-269; *Poems*, vol. 2, pp. 49-50.

53. *Later Poems*, p. 36.

54. MS B2-248; *Poems*, vol. 1, pp. 129.

55. MS A5-3; *Poems*, vol. 1, p. 74.

56. *Letters*, p. 156.

57. Ian Jack, *English Literature 1815-32* (London: Oxford University Press, 1963), p. 137.

58. Edmund Blunden, "John Clare," *Athenaeum*, March 5, 1920, p. 298.

59. "The Moorehens Nest," *Selected Poems*, pp. 79-82.

60. MS A54-269; *Poems*, vol. 2, pp. 49-50.

61. MS A21-53; *Poems,* vol. 1, pp. 446-8.
62. *Selected Poems,* pp. 79-82.
63. Ibid., pp. 91-3.
64. MS A42-125; *Prose,* p. 228.
65. *Selected Poems,* pp. 79-82.
66. MS B2-149a, *Poems,* vol. 1, p. 275.
67. "Expression," MS B2-149a; *Poems,* vol. 1, p. 275.
68. "Spring Songs," MS A41-13; *Poems,* vol. 2, p. 121.
69. "Essay on Landscape," *Prose,* p. 213.
70. [The Badger], *Selected Poems,* pp. 84-6.
71. MS 20, II-358; *Poems of Madness,* p. 216.
72. "Wood Pictures in Spring," *Selected Poems,* p. 127.
73. Prose Fragment, *Prose,* p. 222.
74. *Letters,* p. 133.
75. *Selected Poems,* pp. 144-5.
76. *Letters,* p. 132.
77. "Dawning of Genius," MSS 4-38; *Poems,* vol. 1, pp. 69-70.
78. *Letters,* p. 109.
79. *Prose,* p. 32.
80. *Letters,* p. 50.
81. William Jerom, "Reminiscences of Clare," *TLS,* Dec. 27, 1941, p. 657.
82. *Letters,* p. 75.
83. *Prose,* p. 52.
84 *Letters,* pp. 47 and 143.
85. Ibid., pp. 212-13.
86. It appears in MSS A31, A50, A53, and A54. Accurate dating of these drafts is impossible. The order I have assumed here is based on improvements and additions which are evident from one draft to another. Even without this particular order, however, the drafts demonstrate the extent of Clare's revisions. This "first" draft is from a loose sheet in MS A53.
87. From another loose sheet in MS A53.
88. MSS A50-R37 and A54-366.
89. *Selected Poems,* p. 160.
90. MS 20, I-45; *Poems,* vol. 2, p. 433.
91. *Prose,* p. 225.
92. MSS A54-399; *Poems,* vol. 2, p. 124.

Chapter Three

1. *Prose,* p. 23.
2. Storey, pp. 17ff.
3. MS 1-90; *Poems,* vol. 1, pp. 60-4.

4. MS 3-194; *Poems*, vol. 1, pp. 181-8.

5. MS B2-251a; *Poems*, vol. 1, pp. 75-6.

6. MS 1-20; *Poems*, vol. 1, pp. 31-5.

7. MS 1-151; *Poems*, vol. 1, pp. 84-5.

8. *Selected Poems*, pp. 134-7.

9. MS A54-259; *Poems*, vol. 2, pp. 51-5.

10. MS A40-90; *Poems*, vol. 2, pp. 15-16.

11. MS A54-431; *Poems*, vol. 2, p. 123.

12. All subsequent quotations are from *The Shepherd's Calendar*, eds. Eric Robinson and Geoffrey Summerfield (London: Oxford University Press, 1964).

13. "Introduction," *The Shepherd's Calendar*, p. xiv.

14. John Barrell, *The Idea of Landscape and the Sense of Place 1730-1840* (Cambridge: Cambridge University Press, 1972), p. 169.

15. Storey, p. 94.

16. Ibid., p. 107.

17. Ibid., p. 88.

18. MSS A54-254; *Poems*, vol. 2, pp. 259-61.

19. *Selected Poems*, pp. 100-104.

20. MSS A40-197 and A57-R84; *Poems*, vol. 2, pp. 266-8.

21. *Later Poems*, p. 224.

22. MS 20, II-11; *Poems of Madness*, p. 166.

23. MS 10-end flyleaf; *Poems of Madness*, p. 190.

Chapter Four

1. *Prose*, p. 63.

2. MS A40-51a.

3. *Prose*, p. 62.

4. J. W. and Anne Tibble, *John Clare: A Life*, rev. ed. (London: Michael Joseph, 1972), p. 161.

5. *Letters*, p. 330.

6. On Shakespeare see *Prose*, p. 105; on Milton, *Prose*, p. 109; on Drayton and Spenser, *Prose*, p. 113; and on Surrey, *Letters*, p. 256.

7. MSS 1-24a and A3-99. MS1 is quoted here.

8. MS 5-47. He incorporated other changes, notably a revision of line eight to read "Huge size! to thine—is strange indeed to me," from an intermediate draft in MS A3.

9. "The Moon," MSS 5-117; A3-62. "Evening," MSS 1-134; 5-104; A3-136. "The Glow-worm," MSS 5-30; A3-99.

10. MSS 4-91; 5-51; A3-98.

11. MS A3-63.

12. *Letters*, p. 134.

13. Ibid., p. 142.

14. Ibid., p. 156.

15. MS A3-57; *Poems*, vol. 1, p. 117.

16. *Poems*, vol. 1, p. 117. Tibble appears to have concocted his own poem by incorporating elements of several drafts into his version without following one of them consistently.

17. *Prose*, p. 220.

18. MS B2-248a; *Poems*, vol. 1, p. 129.

19. MS B2-271; *Poems*, vol. 1, p. 277.

20. Thomas R. Frosch, "The Descriptive Style of John Clare," *Studies in Romanticism*, 10 (1971), 145.

21. MS B1-39; *Poems*, vol. 1, p. 123.

22. MS B2-149a; *Poems*, vol. 1, p. 275.

23. MS B2-120; *Poems*, vol. 1, p. 264.

24. MS A40-40; *Poems*, vol. 1, p. 517.

25. MS 17-20; *Poems*, vol. 2, p. 151.

26. Ian Jack, *English Literature 1815-1832* (Oxford: Clarendon, 1963), p. 137.

27. MS A41-1; *Poems*, vol. 2, p. 125.

28. MS 17-12; *Poems*, vol. 2, p. 125.

29. *Selected Poems*, p. 69.

30. Ibid., p. 127.

31. Barrell, p. 149.

32. *Selected Poems*, p. 163.

33. MS A5-10; *Poems*, vol. 1, pp. 69-70.

34. *Selected Poems*, p. 153.

35. MS A54-393; *Poems*, vol. 1, p. 522.

36. *Selected Poems*, p. 160.

37. *Poems*, vol. 2, p. 524n.

38. *Selected Poems*, p. 196.

39. MS 20, II-370; *Poems of Madness*, p. 217.

40. MS D24; *Poems of Madness*, p. 223.

41. *The Letters of William and Dorothy Wordsworth: The Later Years*, ed. E. deSelincourt (Oxford: Clarendon, 1939), vol. 2, p. 653.

Chapter Five

1. *Prose*, p. 135.

2. *Letters*, p. 268.

3. Storey, p. 116.

4. *Letters*, p. 47.

5. *Prose*, p. 12.

6. Ibid., p. 35.

7. *Letters*, p. 40.
8. Ibid., p. 76.
9. *Prose*, p. 51.
10. *Letters*, p. 143.
11. *Prose*, p. 221.
12. *Letters*, p. 97.
13. *Prose*, p. 30.
14. Ibid., p. 30.
15. Ibid., p. 30.
16. *Letters*, p. 57.
17. *Prose*, p. 120.
18. MS 20, I-398; *Poems*, vol. 2, p. 448.
19. M. J. C. Hodgart, *The Ballads* (New York: Norton, 1962), p. 31.
20. MS A54-280; *Poems*, vol. 2, pp. 85-6.
21. Hodgart, p. 34.
22. Ibid., p. 45.
23. C. Day Lewis, *The Lyric Impulse* (London: Chatto and Windus, 1965), p. 3.
24. Ibid., p. 5.
25. *Letters*, pp. 43 and 53.
26. Ibid., p. 60.
27. Ibid., pp. 46 and 119.
28. *Prose*, p. 80; *Letters*, pp. 177, 347-8.
29. *Letters*, p. 63.
30. Ibid.
31. *Letters*, p. 189.
32. Ibid., p. 156.
33. MS 20, II-306; *Poems*, vol. 2, p. 489.
34. MS 20, I-368; *Poems*, vol. 2, pp. 471-2.
35. MS 30-58; *Poems*, vol. 2, p. 264.
36. *Letters*, p. 295.
37. *Poems of Madness*, p. 56.
38. MS 20, I-287; *Poems*, vol. 2, pp. 491-2.
39. MS 20, I-164; *Poems*, vol. 2, p. 493.
40. MS A3-109; *Poems*, vol. 1, p. 24.
41. MS A62-R11.
42. *Prose*, p. 115.
43. *Later Poems*, pp. 233-4.
44. Ibid., p. 249.
45. Ibid., pp. 273-4.
46. MS 20, I-82; *Poems*, vol. 1, p. 467.
47. *Selected Poems*, pp. 196-7.
48. MS 20, I-22; *Poems of Madness*, p. 129.

49. MS A61–122; *Poems,* vol. 2, p. 374.
50. *Selected Poems,* p. 198.
51. *Later Poems,* p. 229.

Chapter Six

1. In *Poems of Madness.*
2. The Tibbles offer another arrangement in their *Selected Poems* (London: Dent, 1965) on the rather facile assumption that "no purpose seems served by placing stanzas obviously written in the spring of 1841 *after* the lines . . . dated July" (p. 239).
3. Two verses of "I've Wandered Many a Weary Mile" and three stanzas of *Child Harold* are written on the end papers of Clare's copy of *Byron's Works* (1828). Unfortunately, this volume has disappeared from Clare's library in the Northampton Public Library. The other sources referred to are MSS 6, 8, 7, 49, Don.c.64, and Don.a.8, respectively.
4. *Poems of Madness,* p. 16.
5. Ibid., p. 12.
6. Naomi Lewis, "The Green Man," *New Statesman,* May 5, 1956, p. 492.
7. Ibid., p. 493.
8. *Later Poems,* p. 8.
9. Storey, pp. 160, 15, 159, 160.
10. Ibid., p. 164.
11. *Poems of Madness,* p. 16.
12. All quotations from *Child Harold* will be from *Later Poems,* but page numbers will be given only for complete sections of the poem or for passages that might be difficult to locate.
13. *Later Poems,* p. 47.
14. Ibid., p. 56.
15. *Letters,* p. 290.
16. *Later Poems,* p. 41.
17. Ibid., pp. 35–41.
18. Ibid., pp. 42–46.
19. Ibid., pp. 47–52.
20. The real Mary Joyce had died by the time Clare wrote this.
21. *Later Poems,* pp. 52–56.
22. Ibid., pp. 57–61.
23. Ibid., pp. 61–2.
24. Ibid., pp. 62–7.
25. Ibid., pp. 68–9.
26. Ibid., pp. 70–80.

Chapter Seven

1. *Selected Poems*, p. xvii.
2. "The Moorehens Nest," *Selected Poems*, pp. 79–82.
3. *Later Poems*, p. 69.
4. Ibid., p. 151.
5. *Poems of Madness*, pp. 57–8.
6. *Selected Poems*, pp. 112–16.
7. William Wordsworth, *The Prelude* [1805], Book First, lines 649–53.
8. *Prose*, p. 210.

Selected Bibliography

PRIMARY SOURCES

1. Works

Poems Descriptive of Rural Life and Scenery. London: Taylor and Hessey, and E. Drury, 1820.

The Village Minstrel, and Other Poems. 2 vols. London: Taylor and Hessey, and E. Drury, 1821.

The Shepherd's Calendar; with Village Stories, and Other Poems. London: For John Taylor, by James Duncan, 1827.

The Rural Muse, Poems by John Clare. London: Whittaker, 1835.

2. Selected Editions

The Poems of John Clare. Edited by J. W. Tibble. 2 vols. London: Dent, 1935. The most complete collection yet published. Its inaccurate readings, rearrangement of stanzas and lines, and its addition of punctuation and even words, make it unreliable.

The Poems of John Clare's Madness. Edited by Geoffrey Grigson. London: Routledge and Kegan Paul, 1949. Includes many asylum poems not in Tibble's collection, but is inaccurate in reading the manuscripts, both in details and the arrangement of *Child Harold.*

The Shepherd's Calendar. Edited by E. Robinson and G. Summerfield. London: Oxford, 1964. An attractive, readable text which restores Taylor's extensive editorial deletions from Clare's original version and prints both of Clare's versions of "July."

The Later Poems of John Clare. Edited by E. Robinson and G. Summerfield. Manchester: The University Press, 1964. Contains *Child Harold, Don Juan,* and poems from manuscript 110 (now MS19) and the Knight Transcripts, all printed as closely as practical to the way they appear in manuscript.

Clare: Selected Poems and Prose. Edited by E. Robinson and G. Summerfield. London: Oxford, 1966. (New Oxford English Series) The best general introduction to Clare's poetry. A representative selection, reliably edited.

The Letters of John Clare. Edited by J. W. and Anne Tibble. London: Routledge and Kegan Paul, 1951; rpt. New York: Barnes and Noble, 1970. A useful *selection* of the letters, printed without punctuation and corrected spelling, although not without inaccuracies.

The Prose of John Clare. Edited by J. W. and Anne Tibble. London: Routledge and Kegan Paul, 1951; rpt. New York: Barnes and Noble, 1970. Contains Clare's Autobiography, Journal, Natural History Letters, Critical Essays, Journey from Essex, and prose fragments. Follows the same editorial policy as the *Letters.*

Sketches in the Life of John Clare by Himself. Edited by Edmund Blunden. London: Cobden-Sanderson, 1931. Clare's autobiography, written for Taylor in 1821, with Clare's fragmentary comments on the eminent contributors to the *London Magazine* as an appendix.

SECONDARY SOURCES

1. Bibliographies

Crossan, G. D. "John Clare: A Chronological Bibliography." *Bulletin of Bibliography,* 32 (1975), 55-62 and 88. The most complete bibliography of writings on Clare available. Includes books, articles, dissertations, editions, reference works, and a selection of reviews of Clare's works and of writings on Clare. Excludes manuscripts.

A Descriptive Catalogue of The John Clare Collection in Peterborough Museum and Art Gallery. Edited by Margaret Grainger. Peterborough: Peterborough Museum Society, 1973. Lists the manuscripts and memorabilia in the Peterborough collection and indexes titles and first lines.

Catalogue of The John Clare Collection in The Northampton Public Library. [ed. D. Powell]. Northampton: Northampton Public Library, 1964. Lists and describes the manuscripts, portraits, and relics in the Northampton collection as well as the books in Clare's own library. Includes indexes of titles and first lines.

2. Biographies

CHERRY, J. L. *Life and Remains of John Clare.* London: Frederick Warne, 1873. Prints numerous poems, letters, and prose fragments and gives a brief account of his life.

MARTIN, FREDERICK. *The Life of John Clare.* London: Macmillan, 1865; rpt. eds. E. Robinson and G. Summerfield. London: Frank Cass, 1964. Has the advantage over other biographies of being written closer to the period of Clare's life. The second edition corrects several inaccuracies in the first, but retains Martin's very readable text.

TIBBLE, J. W. AND ANNE. *John Clare: A Life.* London: Cobden-Sanderson,

1932; rev. and rpt. London: Michael Joseph, 1972. The major biography. Often sketchy and confusing, it remains an adequate introduction to Clare's life.

TIBBLE, J. W. AND ANNE. *John Clare: His Life and Poetry*. London: Heinemann, 1956. Abbreviated version of their 1932 *Life*, but with added critical comment.

WILSON, JUNE. *Green Shadows: The Life of John Clare*. London: Hodder and Stoughton, 1951. A pedestrian biography.

3.   Criticism

BARRELL, JOHN. *The Idea of Landscape and the Sense of Place 1730-1840*. Cambridge: Cambridge University Press, 1972. Invaluable for its detailed analysis of Clare's unique sense of place and its relationship to the tradition of eighteenth-century landscape poetry, this book also explains Clare's place in social, agricultural, and literary history.

BLOOM, HAROLD. *The Visionary Company*. London: Faber, 1962; rev. and rpt. New York: Cornell University Press, 1971. Loses Clare somewhere in his repeated, but not very illuminating comparisons with Wordsworth and Blake.

BROWNLOW, TIMOTHY. "A Molehill for Parnassus: John Clare and Prospect Poetry." *University of Toronto Quarterly*, 48 (1978), 23-40. Places Clare in the tradition of "prospect poetry," then demonstrates how Clare developed his own vision out of that tradition.

CHILCOTT. TIM. *A Publisher and His Circle: The Life and Work of John Taylor, Keats's Publisher*. London: Routledge and Kegan Paul, 1972. Chapter Four explores the relationship between Taylor and Clare from the publisher's point of view, making several interesting observations on Clare's poetry along the way.

CROSSAN, GREG: *A Relish for Eternity: The Process of Divinization in the Poetry of John Clare*. Salzburg Studies in English Literature no. 53. Salzburg: University of Salzburg, 1976. Finds in Clare "a habit of investing all the preoccupation of his life with religious meaning," and uses this habit as the basis for examining Clare's relationship with the past, nature, women, and poetry.

FROSCH, THOMAS R. "The Descriptive Style of John Clare." *Studies in Romanticism*, 10 (1971), 137-49. Treats Clare's descriptive poems as "acts of powerful confrontation with natural and human mutability."

JACK, IAN. *English Literature 1815-1832*. Oxford: Clarendon, 1963. Contains a brief survey of Clare's life and work, stressing the importance of *The Shepherd's Calendar*, but never pausing long enough to examine any poem in detail.

———. "Poems of John Clare's Sanity." In *Some British Romantics*. Eds. James V. Logan, John E. Jordan, and Northrop Frye. Columbus:

Ohio State U. P., 1966. Argues for *The Shepherd's Calendar* as Clare's greatest work.

LEWIS, CECIL DAY. *The Lyric Impulse.* London: Chatto and Windus, 1965. Treating Clare as "the very type of a lyric poet," Lewis presents a sensitive, but all too brief, insight into that aspect of Clare's work.

MURRY, J. MIDDLETON. *John Clare and Other Studies.* London: Peter Nevill, 1950. Contains two perceptive reviews of Clare's poetry as it appeared in *Poems: Chiefly from Manuscripts* and *Madrigals and Chronicles.*

RICHMOND, KENNETH. *Poetry and the People.* London: Routledge and Kegan Paul, 1947. Exaggerates the pathos of Clare's life, but stresses his roots in the folk tradition.

STOREY, MARK. *The Poetry of John Clare. A Critical Introduction.* London: Macmillan, 1974. The most extensive critical study of Clare, it examines his work, without the limitations of a single focus, in the context of his relationship to earlier poets, his major themes, and his developing technique.

―――. ed. *Clare: The Critical Heritage.* London: Routledge and Kegan Paul, 1973. Contains all the general reader and much the Clare scholar needs to trace the public's response to Clare from 1820 to the present. Besides extracts from Clare's letters it also contains valuable letters from his contemporaries to him.

SWINGLE, L. J. "Stalking the Essential John Clare: Clare in Relation to His Romantic Contemporaries." *Studies in Romanticism,* 14 (1975), 273–84. Examines Clare's "catalogue" technique and attempts to distinguish it from the style of other Romantics.

TODD, JANET M. *In Adam's Garden: A Study of John Clare's Pre-Asylum Poetry.* Gainesville, Florida: University of Florida Press, 1973. Traces Clare's Eden metaphor in some detail and relates Clare's treatment of it to the "Golden Age" motif in earlier poets.

WILLIAMS, RAYMOND. *The Country and the City.* London: Chatto and Windus, 1973. Views Clare's poetry in the light of the changing landscape: "Clare marks the end of pastoral poetry, in the very shock of its collision with actual country experience."

Index

Clare did not always title his poems and often the title he used in manuscript was simply a descriptive term like "Ballad" or "Sonnet." In many cases, therefore, I have used the traditional title supplied by editors from John Taylor to J.W. Tibble. For the songs from *Child Harold* I have used the first line as a title and listed them as subentries under *Child Harold*. Extended discussion or quotation of a poem is indicated by italicized page numbers.

DATE DUE

DEMCO 38-297